The Official Business Owners Guide to Selecting a Business Entity

How Every New and Existing Business Can Choose the Best Entity to Operate Their Business

Larry M. Weinstein, CPA
The Tax Terminator®
Certified Tax Reduction Strategist®

AF809718

9639 Hillcroft, Suite 820
Houston, Texas 77096
(713) 726-1603 voice
(832) 202-2500 fax

Larry@Weinstein-CPA.com

This book presents information that is factual as of the time of publication. The information presented here is of a general nature.

How the IRS rules and regulations should best be applied is different in every taxpayer's unique case. Accordingly, no liability can be assumed in how the information is applied to your particular personal situation.

No client relationship has been created or can be inferred by purchase of this book.

Table of Contents

Why I Wrote This Book

There are many tax strategies that can be implemented by a business owner/taxpayer to help reduce the amount of taxes they must pay.

One of the first and biggest decisions that must be made is how your business will be organized.

Clients who are starting new businesses commonly ask, "Should I incorporate?" or "Should I form an LLC?" There seems to be much information floating around in the media and on the Internet, but it is all in "bits and pieces."

I have not yet found a single source of information that describes all of the forms of business which a taxpayer has to choose from.

For this reason I have taken the time to pull all of the guidelines and information together in a logical framework in one place, to assist business owners in evaluating all of their options.

In this book, I have summarized all of the entities from which a taxpayer has to choose, provided a description of what they are, how they work, their significant tax and non-tax considerations, the advantages and disadvantages of each entity, who the entity is best suited for, and those for whom the entity is not the best option.

I hope that you find the answers you are looking for in this book.

Larry M. Weinstein, CPA
"The Tax Terminator®"
Certified Tax Resolution Specialist®
Houston, Texas

Updated for Tax Cuts and Jobs Act of 1017,
passed December 22, 2017

Introduction

As a taxpayer, whether as an individual or a business owner, there are many things to consider when you begin a new business.

Over your lifetime, taxes are the single largest expenditure that a taxpayer makes. Much more than their mortgage or even their cars.

The Tax Foundation, a Washington, D.C., tax research organization, calculates that Tax Freedom Day®, the day of the year in which taxpayers have earned enough to pay all of their tax obligations, was April 23rd for 2017, and comes around that time in April for any other given year as well. For 2017, the effective tax rate was 28.2% of the nation's income, taken as a whole.

Americans will collectively will spend more on taxes in 2017 than they will on food, clothing, and housing combined!!

One of the biggest challenges you'll face on a regular basis is how to minimize the taxes that you pay.

As a small business owner, you have the opportunity to implement various tax strategies to help you reduce the taxes that you pay. Some of these options can literally save you thousands of tax dollars. And many of these options are unavailable to taxpayers who have a job and are employees, rather than being their own boss.

You must take positive, proactive steps to structure your affairs to legally pay the least amount of tax as possible.

Selecting the form of business entity you choose to operate your business is the single biggest decision you will make. It will have a direct impact on how you operate your business, what benefits you will personally receive, and how much you will pay in tax.

Selecting the best business entity for your business is the sole focus of this book.

Chapter 1

What is Tax Planning?

Tax Planning is the process of evaluating various options and strategies available, to determine when, whether, and how to conduct both business and personal transactions to either reduce or eliminate taxes.

Courts have upheld your right to structure your affairs in a manner that legally lowers your tax liability. Known as tax planning or tax avoidance, this is completely legal.

Tax Evasion, however, is the reduction of tax through illegal, fraudulent means. What distinguishes tax avoidance from tax evasion generally is a result of fraud.

Tax Evasion occurs when you have already incurred a tax but attempt to change the facts, to avoid the resulting tax implications.

Some of the main areas in which taxpayers commit fraud include:

Accounting irregularities, including failure to keep adequate books and records, or reporting less income on one's tax returns than have been reported in the accounting records.

Understating income by failing to report all daily cash receipts or interest and dividends.

Overstating expenses by claiming fictitious expenses or large deductions for which no verification exists.

All of the topics discussed in this book regarding selecting a business entity are perfectly legal strategies and are regularly used in tax planning.

Chapter 2

Selecting the Best Entity for Your Business

Every entity from which you can choose has both tax and non-tax aspects that need to be considered when selecting an entity in which to do business.

Tax considerations include how income is taxed, what taxes are involved, and who is responsible for reporting and paying the tax, among other things.

The 2017 Tax Cuts and Jobs Act includes new rules that make pass-through entities potentially more favorable. Eligible pass-through entities are now allowed to exclude from taxable income, 20% of Qualified Business Income.

Non-tax considerations include how many owners the business can have, the legal standing of the business, legal liability exposure of the business owners, the legal life of the business, and the non-taxable benefits available to the owners.

There are six main structures available under which you

can operate your business: a Sole Proprietorship, a General Partnership, a Limited Partnership, a C Corporation, an S Corporation, or a Limited Liability Company.

Chapter 3

Sole Proprietorship

What is a Sole Proprietorship? By definition, a sole proprietorship is an unincorporated business which is owned by a single person.

Ownership. A sole proprietorship can only be owned by a single person. A person is defined as an individual, not another entity such as a corporation or a partnership.

A business owned by more than one person cannot be operated as a sole proprietorship. Some other form of business entity that allows multiple owners must be used.

Ease of formation. A sole proprietorship is the easiest business entity to form. All a taxpayer must do is: declare you are open for business, and begin business operations. It is generally a good idea to register your business name with the appropriate authority to ensure no one else is using the business name, and to reserve your right to use the selected name.

No formal legally recognized entity. No formal separate

legal entity is required. Thus, there is no legal separation between the proprietor and the business. The income and personal assets of the business owners are treated as those of the sole proprietorship.

Even though there is no formal legal separation of business assets from personal assets, it is suggested your business be operated from a business checking account, separate and distinct from your personal checking account. This makes the accounting process much easier, as all business transactions are segregated from your personal transactions. Additionally, this can potentially limit the IRS looking at personal transactions in the event of an audit.

Tax reporting

No separate tax filing is required for a sole proprietorship. The net income or loss of the sole proprietorship is reported on Schedule C, "Profit or Loss from a Business," which is a separate detailed schedule included on the owner's Federal Income Tax Return (Form 1040).

Pass-Through entity

Schedule C's **ARE** a Pass-Through entity, subject to the 20% Qualified Business Income Exclusion. Certain limitations may apply based upon type of business, taxable income, filing status, personal salary and assets employed in the business.

How is income allocated?

Since there is only one owner in a sole proprietorship, there is no allocation of income. All of the income is reported by the owner.

Tax paying

The sole proprietor pays tax on the personal tax return, Form 1040, of the business owner.

What taxes are involved?
The business's net income is subject to federal income tax. The income of the business is considered self-employment income, and is also subject to self-employment tax. Self-employment tax is analogous to Social Security and Medicare taxes that are paid by employees and their employers, and is calculated at 15.3% of self-employment income.

How is the owner paid?
The owner is paid by taking a distribution of profits. Since all the profits of the business already belong to the owner, the owner simply needs to write a check to himself. This is known as an owner's draw.

Draws are not an expense of the business, and do not serve to reduce taxable income. They are simply how the owner chooses to distribute the profits.

Advantages of a Sole Proprietorship

Very easy to set up—All you need to do is to begin doing business. No formal organization or legal paperwork is required. The IRS is notified of your intention to form a sole proprietorship when you file your tax return and include a Schedule C, on April 15 of the year following the end of your first year of business.

Simplified payroll—There is no need to set up the owner as an employee and write a payroll check, or deal with additional responsibilities such as quarterly payroll tax filings, paying employment taxes, and preparing an annual W-2.

Note: Regardless of the type of entity chosen, if a business has employees, it must meet and follow additional requirements which are beyond the scope of this book.

Pass-through entity—Schedule C's **ARE** a Pass-Through

entity, subject to the 20% Qualified Business Income Exclusion. Certain limitations may apply based upon type of business, taxable income, filing status, personal salary and assets employed in the business.

"Pass-through" of losses—Losses "pass through" to the owner's personal tax return. These losses can be used to offset any other taxable income of the owner. This can be important if the business will be generating losses at the inception of the business.

Tax reporting is simplified—Income and expenses of the business are reported on the tax return of the owner. No separate tax returns for the business need to be prepared.

Of course, if the sole proprietor hires employees, they must comply with all recordkeeping and filing requirements for their employees.

Disadvantages of a Sole Proprietorship

Single owner—A sole proprietorship can only have one owner. If more than one owner is desired, another form of entity must be used.

Taxed on income—The business owner is personally responsible for the tax due on the profits of the business, regardless of whether or not cash was taken out of the business.

Unlimited personal liability—The business owner is subject to unlimited personal liability. The owner is personally liable for all debts and other liabilities and judgments of the business, even if in excess of the amount invested or loaned to the business.

Not only are the assets of the business at risk, but all assets personally owned by the sole proprietor are also subject to the risks of the business.

Difficulty raising capital—It can be much tougher raising capital as a sole proprietor. Capital used in a sole proprietorship is limited to the personal funds contributed by the owner and the ability of the owner to borrow.

Assets of the owner will serve as the primary collateral for loans, which may not be enough for some lenders.

Additionally, the creditworthiness of the owner will be analyzed in making a credit decision.

No continuity of life—Since a sole proprietorship is owned by a single individual, when this individual dies, the business technically ceases to exist. Their heirs may be able to sell the business, but it may be more difficult.

Who Should Operate as a Sole Proprietorship?

A sole proprietorship is usually considered by individuals with businesses that are just beginning operations. Ease of formation and minimal legal expenses are a big plus. There are no expenses of formation, other than registering the business name. If a business is being started on a limited budget, a sole proprietorship may be a good choice.

Businesses that wish to take advantage of the 20% Qualified Business Income Exclusion should choose to operate their business as a Sole Propreitorship.

Many new businesses are not profitable in the first year and generate losses. Losses that are generated by a sole proprietorship can be used by the owner to offset taxable income from other sources such as a working spouse, rental properties, investment income or other employment.

Who Should Not Operate as a Sole Proprietorship

Since sole proprietors can only have a single owner, if there will be more than one owner, another entity must be considered.

Be aware that sole proprietors are responsible for the financial obligations of the business. Additionally, the owner's personal assets are at risk for any business debts or court judgments.

If there could be significant liability exposure, it may be wise to consider another type of entity that will limit the owner's liability.

Chapter 4

General Partnership

What is a General Partnership? A general partnership is an association that is owned by two or more persons to conduct business as co-owners for a profit.

"Persons" is defined as individuals, partnerships, corporations, and limited liability companies (much broader than a sole proprietor).

Ownership. A general partnership is owned by two or more persons. There is no limit to the number of persons who can be owners of a general partnership.

All partners can act as an agent of the partnership for the purpose of conducting its business. All partners are legally bound by the actions of any partner who acts within the scope of the partnership's business.

A single person cannot own a general partnership. A single individual must operate as either a sole proprietor or a single-member limited liability company, a C Corporation, or an S Corporation.

Ease of formation. Like a sole proprietorship, a general partnership is also a relatively easy business entity to form. All the owners need to do is declare they are open for business and to begin operations. It is generally a good idea to register the business name with the local authority to ensure no one is using the name and to reserve your right to use the selected name.

It is also suggested that a partnership agreement be adopted and signed by all of the partners.

Items that should be included in the agreement:

- The term of the partnership
- How changes to the partnership ownership will be handled upon the death, disability, retirement or withdrawal of a partner
- Requirements for the admission of new partners
- How income/losses will be allocated
- How and when partner distributions will be made and how they will be determined
- What the capital contributions of the partners will be and how the partner interests will be divided
- Listing of duties and responsibilities of the partners
- How the partnership will handle management of the partnership

Partnerships are not a formal legally recognized entity. A general partnership is a legal entity, but not formal in the sense that it does not have to be registered with the state.

The personal assets of the partners are treated as available for the settlement of partnership debts. There is no separation between the assets of the partners and the assets of the partnership. Basically, if the partnership gets sued, then the assets of the partners are at risk.

Legal Liability

All partners in a general partnership are jointly and severally liable for the actions of their partners and also for the debts, obligations and liabilities of the partnership.

Joint and several liability means that a creditor can pursue any or all partners to collect on debts. Generally, creditors can pursue ALL partners, to try and obtain a settlement, since there is no formal legal separation of partnership assets from a partner's personal assets.

It is suggested that a partnership maintain a business checking account, separate and distinct from the personal checking accounts of the partners.

Tax Reporting

A separate tax filing is required for a general partnership. The activities of the general partnership are reported on a Form 1065, "U. S. Return of Partnership Income." Allocable partner income or loss is reported to the partners on Schedule K-1, "Partner's Share of Income, Deductions and Credits."

Pass-Through Entity

General Partnerships **ARE** a Pass-Through entity, subject to the 20% Qualified Business Income Exclusion. Certain limitations may apply based upon type of business, taxable income, filing status, personal salary and assets employed in the business.

How is Income Allocated?

Income is allocated on a pro-rata basis (based upon ownership) among the partners. Generally, the net income or losses are allocated to the partners based upon the ownership percentages, unless the partnership agreement indicates otherwise.

However, a general partnership is very flexible in how income and losses can be allocated to the partners. Income and losses are not required to be allocated based upon the percentage ownership of the partners. Income and losses can be allocated to partners in any manner in which they agree, as long as the allocation has real economic effect and is not being done to evade taxes.

For example, all of the losses can be allocated to one partner and all of the profits can be allocated to another partner. Or an allocation can be made on a 75/25% basis, when in fact, there are only two partners who each own 50%. The only requirement is that the entire amount of income or loss be allocated to someone and that evasion of tax is not the reason for the allocation.

Tax Paying

The general partnership is a tax reporting, but not a tax paying entity. Income is allocated to each individual partner, who must report and pay taxes on their pro-rata portion of the income or loss on their personal tax return.

What Taxes Are Involved?

The partner's reported net income is subject to federal

income tax. Because the income of the general partners is considered self-employment income, it is also subject to self-employment tax. Self-employment tax is analogous to Social Security and Medicare taxes that are paid by employees and their employers.

How Are the Owners Paid?

A partner can receive two types of income from the partnership: guaranteed payments and cash distributions.

Partners can be paid guaranteed payments from the partnership for their efforts. Guaranteed payments to partners are an expense of the partnership and reduce the net income of the partnership, and the amount of income reported to the partners. Guaranteed payments to partners are reported on Schedule K-1, and also have to be reported on a W-2.

Partners can also receive cash distributions from the partnership. Partnership distributions are usually considered to be a distribution of income, similar to owner draws taken by a sole proprietor.

Accordingly, partnership distributions are not considered income to the shareholder and are not subject to self-employment tax.

Partners can have distributions made in any amount agreed to by the partners, subject to cash availability.

Partnership distributions up to the amount of the partners' capital account are considered a return of capital and are not taxable.

Distributions in excess of the balance in their partners' capital account would be reported as capital gain income.

Advantages of a General Partnership

Relatively easy to set up—All that a general partnership must do is to begin operations. No formal organization or legal paperwork is required.

A newly formed general partnership must obtain an Employer Identification Number (EIN) by completing Form SS-4, "Application for Employer Identification Number." This identifying number will be used by the partnership on all of their tax filings.

Multiple owners—By definition, a general partnership must consist of two or more partners (owners). An unlimited number of partners can be in a general partnership.

Easier to raise capital—Having more than one partner can allow multiple partners to contribute capital to the business and have the ability to borrow money on behalf of the business. It may be easier to get a loan with more people signing as responsible parties.

More depth of management—Having more than one owner diversifies the management talent available to the business. The more partners involved, the more talent, experience, and skill-sets available to help grow and run the business.

Simplified payroll—Partners are not employees so there are no payroll tax filings, employment taxes and no need to prepare annual W-2s.

Of course, if the partnership hires employees, the partnership must comply with all recordkeeping and filing requirements for their employees.

Pass-through entity—General Partnerships **ARE** a Pass-Through entity, subject to the 20% Qualified Business

Income Exclusion. Certain limitations may apply based upon type of business, taxable income, filing status, personal salary and assets employed in the business.

"Pass-through" of losses—Losses "pass through" to the partner's personal tax return. This can be important if the partnership is generating losses. These losses can be used to offset any other taxable income of the partner, subject to the following limitations.

Limitation on losses—Losses can only be deducted up to the amount of one's basis in the partnership.

> <u>Basis in the Partnership is calculated as</u>
> Cash initially contributed to the partnership
> + Cash contributed after initial contribution
> + Value of property contributed to the partnership
> + Debt personally guaranteed by partner
> + Income that was taxed to you in the past, not received
> - Partnership distribution received
> <u>- Losses passed through to you</u>
> Adjusted basis of partnership

Deductibility of health insurance premiums—Partners may deduct up to 100% of health insurance premiums for themselves and their family, limited to the extent of profit reported by the partner. The deduction is an adjustment to income on the partners Form 1040, rather than a business expense.

No double taxation of profits—Since a partnership is not a tax paying entity, tax is only paid by the individual partners. All profits flow through to the partners who pay their portion of the tax on their personal tax returns.

Disadvantages of a General Partnership

More management—Although many may consider having more partners and the additional talent that goes along with more partners as an asset, this may not always be the case.

Human nature will always come into play.vSometimes disagreements will arise concerning business decisions that can be tough to settle.

Complaints about money and draws—There can be major disagreements between the partners concerning money. This can be the single largest problem faced by general partnerships. More partnerships break up over money than all other reasons combined.

Reasons for disagreements can include uneven distributions of profit based upon capital contributed, effort expended or results achieved.

A well-drafted partnership agreement should thoroughly address how partnership distributions will be handled.

Taxed on income—Partners are personally responsible for the tax due on their pro-rata profits of the business, regardless of whether cash was distributed from the business.

However, it is quite common for the partnership to make distributions to the partners (which are not considered income) to cover the tax liability incurred by the partners, attributable to partner income.

Unlimited personal liability—Partners are subject to unlimited personal liability. All partners are personally liable for all debts and liabilities and judgments of the partnership. This includes any actions taken by any other partners on behalf of the partnership.

This may the single biggest disadvantage of a general partnership.

Difficulty raising capital—It can be tough raising capital as a partnership. The assets of the partners and the partnership serve as the primary collateral for loans, which may not satisfy some lenders' requirements.

No continuity of life—A general partnership is owned by the partners. When there is a 50% or greater change in ownership, the partnership technically ceases to exist. A new partnership must be established for the remaining partners, which would entail additional paperwork and possible legal fees.

Who is a General Partnership Best Suited For?

A general partnership might be considered by individuals with businesses that are just commencing operations.

Businesses that wish to take advantage of the 20% Qualified Business Income Exclusion should choose to operate their business as a General Partnership.

Many new businesses are not profitable in the first year or two, and generate losses that can be used by the partners to reduce their taxable income from other sources of income such as a working spouse, rental properties, or investment income.

If there will be more than one owner, the owners may want to consider a general partnership. If there will be only one owner, another entity should be considered.

There are no expenses of formation, other than registering the business name. A general partnership is a good choice if the owners are working with a limited budget.

Who Should Not Operate as a General Partnership

If there is significant potential for liability exposure in your chosen business, you may want to consider another form of business with limited liability exposure for the owners, such as a corporation or limited liability company. Potential liability exposure could include anything from someone slipping and falling on your property to an employee suing you.

Be aware that all general partners are responsible for all financial obligations of the business. Additionally, the partner's personal assets are at risk for any business debts or court judgments. If being held responsible for the actions of your partner(s) concerns you, you may want to consider a different type of entity.

I suggest that you know your partners very well before going into business with them. Because you will be held responsible for the actions of your partner, you should ensure that any potential partners are trustworthy and exercise good judgment. Make sure, and do a thorough background check on your partner. Hopefully, you'll know the people you're going into business with.

Ideally, you should find a partner who brings a different set of skills to the business than you do. For example, if you are exceptionally talented in marketing, choose a partner with complementary skills such as finance or operations.

The truth contained in an age-old saying, "Two heads are better than one," can be very helpful in a small business partnership.

Finally, having a buy-sell agreement already in place will help the partners amicably end the partnership when they decide to do so.

Chapter 5

Limited Partnership

A limited partner is a partnership which is formed by two or more persons. A limited partner has some attributes of a general partnership and some attributes of a corporation.

There must be at least one or more general partners. There can be one or more limited partners.

General partners are responsible for managing the partnership's business activities. General partners have unlimited liability for all debts and obligations of the partnership.

Limited partners are generally only liable for the amount of their initial capital contribution/investment and any subsequent investments.

They are not liable for the debts and obligations of the limited partnership.

Limited partners should not in any way participate in management. If a limited partner participates in management, or is significantly involved in the operations of the business, they may lose their limited liability protection.

The formation and operation of a limited partnership requires more formality than does the formation and operation of a general partnership.

Generally, a limited partnership must file a certificate of limited partnership with the Secretary of State and must have a written partnership agreement. These documents govern the business operations of the entity. A written partnership agreement is strongly suggested.

Tax reporting
Similar to a general partnership, a separate tax filing is required for a limited partnership. The net income or loss of the limited partnership is reported on Form 1065, "U. S. Return of Partnership Income." Partner income or loss is reported to the partners on Schedule K-1, "Partner's Share of Income, Deductions and Credits."

Pass-through entity
Limited Partnerships **ARE** a Pass-Through entity, subject to the 20% Qualified Business Income Exclusion. Certain limitations may apply based upon type of business, taxable income, filing status, personal salary and assets employed in the business.

How is income allocated?
Income is allocated on a pro-rata basis among the partners, based upon the ownership percentages.

However, a limited partnership is very flexible in how income and losses can be allocated to the partners. Income and losses are not required to be allocated based upon the percentage ownership of the partners. Income and losses can be allocated to partners in any manner in which they agree, as long as the allocation has real economic effect and is not being done to evade taxes.

For example, all of the losses can be allocated to one partner and all of the profits can be allocated to another partner. Or an allocation can be made on a 75/25 % basis, when in fact, there are only two partners who each own 50%. The only requirement is that the entire amount of income or loss be allocated to someone and that evasion of tax is not the reason for the allocation.

Tax paying

A limited partnership is a tax reporting, not a tax paying, entity. Income is allocated to each individual partner, who then report and pay taxes on their pro-rata portion of the income on their personal tax return.

What taxes are involved?

For all partners, the reported net income is subject to federal income tax.

Income of the general partner(s) is considered self-employment income, and is also subject to self-employment tax, if the general partner(s) is an individual. Self-employment tax is analogous to Social Security and Medicare taxes that are paid by employees and their employers.

Income of the limited partners is not considered self-employment income, and thus not subject to self-employment tax. The income would also be subject to passive activity rules.

How is the owner paid?

A partner can receive two types of income from the partnership. The general partner can be paid "guaranteed payments to partners" for effort expended, analogous to wages.

Guaranteed payments to general partners are an expense

of the partnership and reduce the net income of the partnership, and the amount of income reported to the partners. Guaranteed payments to partners are reported on the partner's Schedule K-1.

Since limited partners cannot actively participate in the operation of the business, they cannot be paid guaranteed payments for the services they perform.

Partners can also receive cash distributions from the partnership. Partnership distributions are usually considered to be a distribution of income, similar to owner draws for a sole proprietor.

Partners can have distributions made in any amount agreed to by the partners, subject to cash availability.

Partnership distributions up to the amount of the partner's capital account are considered a return of capital and not taxable. Partnership distributions that are in excess of the balance in their capital account would be reported as capital gain income and are taxable.

Advantages of a Limited Partnership

Multiple owners—There can be an unlimited number of owners. The only requirement is that there must be at least one general partner and at least one limited partner. Usually, there is only one general partner, but there can be more. The number of limited partners is usually only limited by the amount of money needed by the partnership.

Limited liability—Limited partners' liability exposure is limited to their investment in the partnership. Limited partners are not liable for the debts and general obligations of the partnership.

Limited partners should not participate in management or perform significant personal services for the partnership.

Partnership distributions—Partners may receive cash distributions without affecting their tax liability. Partners are liable for the tax on their pro-rata share of the partnership's profits, whether or not they are distributed. At a minimum many partnerships distribute enough money to allow the partners to pay for the partners' taxes on the partnership income.

Centralized management—Management is centralized under the control of the general partner. Limited partners are not and should not be involved in the operations of the business. Limited partners basically serve as investors only.

Raising capital—There is no limit to the number of limited partners. The amount of capital raised by the limited partnership is only limited by the number of limited partners that can be recruited for the capital requirements of the limited partnership. This can be one of the main reasons for using a limited partnership to raise money for businesses requiring large investments.

Continuity of life—Unlike general partnerships, most limited partnerships don't terminate on the death or disability of a limited partner.

However, if a general partner dies or becomes disabled, this could become a problem unless the partnership agreement allows limited partners to recruit or assign a new general partner.

Pass-through entity—Limited Partnerships **ARE** a Pass-Through entity, subject to the 20% Qualified Business Income Exclusion. Certain limitations may apply based upon type of business, taxable income, filing status, personal salary and assets employed in the business.

"Pass-through" of income—Partnerships are tax reporting and not tax paying. Income and losses of the partnerships are "passed through" to the partners who pay tax at their individual rates. Losses can be used to offset other taxable income of the partners.

Disadvantages of a Limited Partnership

Limited marketability—There usually isn't a strong secondary market for limited partnership interests. This can make the sale of a limited partnership interest difficult.

Usually, in the cases of privately-held limited partnerships, the only people interested in buying your partnership interest are the other limited partners and/or the general partner. (If it's a publicly traded limited partnership, the scenario would be different.)

Normally, the general partner must approve the sale of a partnership interest to another party.

Unlimited liability for the general partner—The general partner has unlimited liability for the debts and obligations of the limited partnership. One of the ways around this is that the general partner can be organized as either a corporation or a limited liability company, which enjoy limited liability protection.

More costly to organize and administer—Because most people usually consult an attorney to help set this up, it is frequently costly to establish a limited partnership due to the filing of "Certificate of Limited Partnership" and the complexity of the partnership agreement, and the requirement for good accounting and proper tax reporting to the partners.

No control over the general partner—General partners control the day-to-day activities of the partnership. Limited partners have little control over how the general partner operates the business.

Limited partners may not participate in management— If limited partners participate in management they may lose their limited liability status. Businesses which require the personal services of limited partners should consider other types of entities.

Passive loss limitations—Limited partnerships are generally treated as passive activities. You may be limited as an individual in how much or whether you will be able to deduct the losses generated by your partnership interest.

Passive losses can only be offset against passive income. "Passive activities" are those in which you're generally not involved in the operations of the business yourself, but where you are an "investor" instead. If your passive losses are limited, then they are written off against passive income, or they can be carried over to subsequent years when you might be able to utilize them, or until the investment is sold or otherwise disposed of.

Who is a Limited Partnership Best Suited For?

Limited partnerships can be very useful entities. They limit the liability of limited partners and can be used to raise significant amounts of capital. However, limited partners can not be actively involved in the business.

Businesses that wish to take advantage of the 20% Qualified Business Income Exclusion should choose to operate their business as a Limited Partnership.

Businesses that own, develop, and operate real estate or drilling and mining activities can most effectively utilize limited partnerships. This is because limited partners can make an investment and not be subject to all the underlying liabilities involved in owning and running the partnership.

Again, a limited partner of the business may not be directly involved with running the business, because this is being done by the general partner.

Who Should Not Use a Limited Partnership?

Limited partnerships should not be used by entities in which all partners render services to the business or will be actively involved in the management of the business.

Active participation by limited partners in their businesses will nullify their limited liability status.

Chapter 6

C Corporation

A corporation is a legal entity, formed under state law, that exists separate and apart from its owners and shareholders.

The word incorporate means to create a "separate body." Corporations have all the rights and powers of a "natural person" (as opposed to a "fictitious person"), including the right to conduct lawful business, to own property, to enter into contracts, to be responsible for its own debts, and to sue and be sued in its corporate name.

Corporations are a "fictitious person" that are granted their legal status by filing the appropriate legal documents such as the Articles of Incorporation and by-laws with the Secretary of State in the state of organization.

Since the business is a separate legal entity, owners of the business, called shareholders, have legal liability protection.

Generally, all debts and obligations of the corporation remain exclusively with the corporation, and not the shareholders. The liability of the shareholders is limited to the amount of money invested into the corporation.

A corporation, by default, is called a C Corporation. C Corporations are named after Subchapter C of the Internal Revenue Code.

Tax reporting

A C Corporation is a tax reporting and tax paying entity. A separate tax filing is required for a C Corporation. The net income or loss of a C Corporation is reported on a Form 1120, "U.S. Corporation Income Tax Return."

NOT a Pass-through entity

C Corporations **ARE NOT** a Pass-Through entity. C Corporations are the ONLY type of entity **NOT** subject to the 20% Qualified Business Income Exclusion. If you wish to take advantage of the 20% Qualified Business Income Exclusion, a C Corporation would **NOT** be the correct choice.

How is income allocated?

There is no income allocation for a C Corporation, such as with "pass-through" entities. All income of the corporation is the responsibility of the corporation.

Tax paying

A C Corporation reports and pays taxes on 100% of its income. Losses not tax deductible currently by the corporation are carried forward or backward to offset profits.

What taxes are involved?

A C Corporation's reported net income is subject to Federal Corporate Income Tax. This corporate income tax is separate from the federal income tax paid by the shareholders on their individual income tax return and is not the responsibility of the shareholders.

How is the owner paid?

A shareholder/owner of the corporation can receive two

types of income from the corporation. Shareholders can be paid wages from the corporation, just like any other employee.

If a shareholder works for and provides services for a C Corporation, they are an employee of the corporation and must be paid wages for the services that they perform.

Wages paid to shareholders are an expense of the corporation and reduce the net income of the corporation. Wages paid to shareholders are reported on a Form W-2, just like wages paid to any other employee.

Shareholders can also receive dividends from the corporation. Dividends paid to shareholders are considered to be a distribution of retained earnings and are not tax deductible by the corporation. However, dividends are considered income to the shareholder and included in the shareholder's taxable income, thus causing double taxation, once at the corporate level and once at the shareholder level.

Advantages of a C Corporation

Limited liability—The single greatest non-tax reason to establish a corporation is limited liability protection.

When the corporation is properly set up and the owners adhere to the corporate formalities, a shareholder's liability is limited to their investment in the corporation. Because a corporation is a fictitious person, it is responsible for its own debts and obligations. They are not debts and obligations of the shareholders.

Reasons for losing the limited liability status of the corporation include fraud, malpractice, and failure to adhere to the corporate formalities, such as having annual shareholder meetings and documenting these meetings in the corporate minutes.

Transferability of ownership—Unlike general partnerships or limited partnerships, an owner in a C Corporation can usually sell his or her stock without the approval of the corporation or other stockholders. However, in many non-public small corporations, shareholder agreements are in place which may restrict the transfer of shares.

Continuity after the death of shareholders/owners—If a shareholder dies, the corporation continues to exist. Generally, the heirs of the shareholder will inherit their shares, or they will pass in accordance with the deceased's will.

Ease of raising capital—If you need to raise additional cash for your business, you can sell authorized, but previously unissued, shares of stock in your C Corporation to outside investors. These investors are investing money in your business, but may not normally be involved in the operations of the business.

Large businesses traded on a national stock exchange are usually organized as C Corporations and can sell as many shares to the public as are authorized.

Specialized management—Corporations may hire as many officers and managers as they can afford. A corporation can hire people to handle many different aspects of the business, such as finance, marketing, and operations.

Accumulation of capital—Unlike pass-through entities, corporations are subject to their own tax rates. This allows corporations to pay tax on their earnings and accumulate capital within the corporation. There is no requirement for a corporation to pay a dividend.

Capital can be accumulated for any valid business purpose such as expansion of the business, purchase of inventory, or marketing.

Tax-free benefits for employees—Employees of C Corporations can receive fringe benefits on a tax-free basis. These benefits can include health insurance, disability insurance, and group term life insurance up to $50,000.

Ordinary loss on sale of stock—If planned correctly during the formation of the corporation, you can elect for the stock in your corporation to be classified as small business stock (section 1244). Losses realized on the sale of small business stock are considered ordinary losses, and can be written off directly against any other income of the shareholder in the year of the loss.

Normally, losses on the sale of stock (capital losses) are limited to a net capital loss deduction of $3,000 per year. Any losses greater than $3,000 must be carried forward to future years to be deducted, with the same $3,000 per year limitation.

The requirements to qualify as Small Business Stock are as follows:

> 1) The stock was issued by a domestic corporation which was a "small business corporation" at the time the stock was issued;
>
> 2) The stock was issued by such corporation for money or other property (other than stock and securities); and
>
> 3) The aggregate amount received for the stock was less than one million dollars; and
>
> 4) The corporation, during the period of its five most recent taxable years ending before the date the loss on such stock was sustained, derived more than 50% of its aggregate gross receipts from sources other than royalties,

rents, dividends, interests, annuities, and sales or exchanges of stocks or securities.

Exclusion of gain on small business stock—Shareholders of small business stock may exclude up to 50% of the gain they realize on the disposition of their stock. To qualify, the stock must have been issued after August 10, 1993 and held by the shareholder for more than five years.

Disadvantages of a C Corporation

Double taxation—C Corporations report and pay their own taxes. This tax must be paid by the corporation. Dividends paid out to shareholders are taxed to the shareholders as dividend income when received. This is considered "double taxation."

Some business owners reduce their corporate income (and corporate income tax) to zero, by monitoring the income at year end, and paying out enough in bonus and salaries to the owners to reduce the corporate income tax to zero.

This serves to reduce corporate income tax and shifts the income tax to the shareholder and mitigates "double taxation" of corporate income.

In some instances, it may be beneficial to incur the "double taxation" by taking advantage of the lower corporate tax rates. For example, if a corporation is in a lower tax bracket than an individual, then the tax to the corporation would be less. Ultimately, I still consider this to be "double taxation," and I don't see it done very often in the real world.

All of this takes proper accounting and planning, which increases the costs of maintaining the corporation.

NOT a Pass-through entity—C Corporations **ARE NOT** a Pass-Through entity. C Corporations are the ONLY type of entity **NOT** subject to the 20% Qualified Business Income Exclusion. If you wish to take advantage of the 20% Qualified Business Income Exclusion, a C Corporation would **NOT** be the correct choice.

No "pass-through" of losses—Because the corporation is a separate tax reporting and tax paying entity, any losses generated by the corporation can only be used by the corporation. There is no tax benefit to the shareholders.

Losses do not "pass through" to the shareholders to be used to offset their personal income. Thus, in the early years of the business or in years in which the business generates a loss, there is no tax benefit to the shareholders/owners for losses generated.

Additional paperwork—Properly operating a C Corporation involves much additional paperwork. Corporate formalities that must be addressed include annual shareholder meetings, board meetings to elect officers, and approval of major issues within the corporation such as debt, and approval of major purchases and business strategies. These must all be formally documented in the corporate minutes.

Additionally, separate and distinct bank accounts in the corporation's name must be maintained for the corporation, as well as a proper accounting system and books and records.

More expensive to form—A corporation must pay its Secretary of State an incorporation fee to be established.

Added administrative costs—Operating a corporation involves preparing a corporate income tax return, including all of the accounting required to prepare the return. A corporation has employees, which involves preparing payroll, and preparing quarterly and annual payroll reports.

Potential tax issues—Corporations have many potential traps established to defeat potential abuses by taxpayers.

Additional taxes can be assessed for:

- Personal holding companies—Corporations with excessive unearned income such as interest, dividends and capital gains.
- Accumulated earnings tax—Corporations with excessive accumulated earnings that have not been paid out in dividends.
- Personal service corporations—Corporations which render personal services such as medicine, law, accounting, engineering and consulting are assessed a flat 35% tax on all income.

Who Should Operate as a C Corporation?

Business owners who have significant potential liability exposure and desire to protect themselves.

Businesses that **WISH** to take advantage of the 20% Qualified Business Income Exclusion.

Businesses that need to accumulate capital for inventory, marketing, and expansion.

Businesses that expect to go public sometime in the future.

Businesses that want tax deductible fringe benefits including health insurance.

Who Should Not Operate as a C Corporation

Businesses that determine they do not need limited liability protection.

Businesses that offer personal services that would be classified as a Personal Service Corporation, as defined above.

Businesses that cannot afford the cost of incorporation, the cost of accounting, and the additional costs of maintaining the corporate documents.

Chapter 7

S Corporation

S Corporations are corporations organized just like C Corporations. They are granted their legal status (known as a charter) by the Secretary of State in their state of incorporation. S Corporations have the same corporate formalities as C Corporations such as stockholder meetings, board of directors meetings, and the keeping of corporate minutes.

However, an S Corporation is a hybrid entity. It has the limited liability structure of a corporation, but it is taxed like a partnership. S Corporations are named after Subchapter S of the Internal Revenue Code.

S Corporation status must be elected after forming the entity by filing a Form 2553, "Election by a Small Business Corporation." This election must be agreed to and signed by all shareholders.

The qualification for being an S Corporation are:

- The corporation must have 100 or fewer shareholders. A husband and wife count as only one shareholder.

- The corporation must be a domestic corporation formed in the United States. Corporations formed in other countries cannot elect S status.
- Only individuals, estates and certain types of limited trusts can be shareholders. Partnerships, other corporations and most trusts can't own stock in an S Corporation.
- All stock must be owned by a U.S. resident or U.S. citizen. Foreign investors are not allowed.
- There can be only a single class of stock. If you have more than one class of stock, you can't be an S Corporation.

You must meet all of the above requirements at the time the S Corporation election is made, and continue to meet them to be an S Corporation.

If you meet all five requirements at the inception of the business, and violate even one of the requirements at any time in the future, your S Corporation status terminates on the date of the violation.

Since all business is conducted in the name of the corporation, owners of the business, called shareholders, have limited liability protection. All debts and obligations of the corporation remain exclusively with the corporation, and not the shareholders. The liability of the shareholders is limited to the amount of money invested in the corporation and any debts personally guaranteed.

Tax reporting

A separate tax filing is required for an S Corporation. The net income or loss of an S Corporation is reported on a Form 1120S, "U.S. Income Tax Return for an S Corporation."

Pass-through entity

S Corporations **ARE** a Pass-Through entity, subject to the 20% Qualified Business Income Exclusion. Certain limitations may apply based upon type of business, taxable income, filing status, personal salary and assets employed in the business.

How is income allocated?

Income is allocated on a pro-rata basis among the shareholders. The net income or losses are allocated to the shareholders, based upon ownership percentages. There is no flexibility in the allocation of profit and loss.

Tax paying

An S Corporation is a tax reporting, but not a tax paying entity. No tax is paid by the corporation. The income is allocated to each individual shareholder, who each report and pay taxes on the pro-rata portion of their income on their personal tax return.

What taxes are involved?

Shareholders pay Federal Income Tax and Social Security on all wages they receive.

Income allocated to the shareholders is not considered self-employment income, and is not subject to self-employment tax.

How is the owner paid?

A shareholder/owner of an S Corporation can receive two types of income from the corporation. Shareholders can be paid wages from the corporation, like any other employee.

If a shareholder works for and provides services for an S Corporation, they are an employee of the corporation and must be paid wages for the services that they perform.

Wages paid to shareholders are reported on a Form W-2, similar to wages paid to any other employee.

Wages paid to shareholders are an expense of the corporation and reduce the net income of the corporation.

Shareholders may also receive shareholder distributions from the S Corporation. Shareholder distributions are made in accordance with the shareholder's percentage of ownership.

Shareholder cash distributions are considered to be a distribution of income and are not a tax deductible expense of the corporation.

Shareholder cash distributions are not considered income to the shareholder and are not subject to self-employment tax.

Advantages of an S Corporation

No double taxation—S Corporations report their own income, however the taxes are paid by shareholders on their personal returns. There is no income tax at the corporate level, such as with a C Corporation.

Continuity of life—If a shareholder of an S Corporation dies, the S Corporation continues to exist. There is no need to reform the corporation upon the death of the shareholder. Generally, the heirs of the shareholder would receive their shares through inheritance,or they will pass in accordance with the will.

Pass-through entity—S Corporations **ARE** a Pass-Through entity, subject to the 20% Qualified Business Income Exclusion. Certain limitations may apply based upon type of business, taxable income, filing status, personal salary and assets employed in the business.

"Pass-through" of losses—Losses "pass through" to the shareholders based upon their pro-rata share of stock ownership and can be used to offset other income of the shareholder.

Shareholders are compensated for their work with wages—If a shareholder works in the business, they must be paid fair and reasonable wages for the work performed. These wages are considered earned income and are taxable to the shareholder. This earned income can qualify you for participation in a retirement plan which is based on earned income.

Shareholders can receive cash distributions—Shareholders can be paid a profit distribution, commonly called a shareholder's distribution. Shareholders' distributions are not a deductible expense of the corporation, and do not reduce corporate income nor are they taxable income to the shareholder.

It is common for S Corporations to make cash distributions to the shareholders at least in the amount of tax paid by the shareholder on their pro-rata share of the corporate income.

Limited liability—S Corporations have the same limited liability protection as C Corporations. Of course all legal formalities must be adhered to such as board meetings, shareholder meetings, and the keeping of corporate records.

Easier accounting and tax planning—Because there is no tax at the corporate level, the double taxation involved with C Corporations is eliminated. This elimination of one level of tax makes planning simpler.

Ordinary loss on sale of stock—Similar to a C Corporation, an election can be made for the stock in your corporation to be classified as small business stock (section 1244).

Losses on the sale of small business stock are considered an ordinary loss, and can be written off directly against any other income of the shareholder in the year of the loss, rather than the limitation of the net capital loss deduction of $3,000 per year.

See C Corporations for requirements of being classified Section 1244 Small Business Stock.

Ability to split income—Income is allocated to shareholders based upon their pro-rata share of stock ownership. Having family members who are in lower tax brackets become co-owners of the business may allow some income to be taxed at their lower rates, thereby lowering income tax payments.

Exclusion of gain on small business stock—Shareholders of small business stock may exclude up to 50% of the gain they realize on the disposition of their stock. To qualify, the stock must have been issued after August 10, 1993, and held by the shareholder for more than five years.

Specialized management—Similar to a C Corporation, S Corporations can also have centralized management. All

Corporations have a board of directors whose job is to oversee management on behalf of the shareholders.

Less potential for tax traps—Because an S Corporation is a "pass-through" entity and does not have its own tax rates nor pay its own tax as a C Corporation does, it is less likely to encounter the tax problems that are possible with C Corporations. Some of these problems can include being classified as a Personal Services Corporation or a Personal Holding Company, or having the Accumulated Earnings Tax assessed.

Disadvantages of an S Corporation

Restrictions on qualifying for S Corporation status—

There are restrictions that must be met to qualify as an S Corporation. If you don't meet these requirements at the inception of the business, or at any time in the future, a business cannot operate as an S Corporation and the election will be terminated.

Increased accounting cost—An accurate accounting must be made to prepare the corporate tax return and to properly allocate income and expense to the shareholders.

Additional paperwork—Because an S Corporation is a legal corporation, operating an S Corporation involves additional paperwork, as does a C Corporation.

Corporate formalities that must be addressed include annual shareholders meetings, board meetings to elect officers, and approval of major issues within the corporation such as debt and approval of major purchases and business strategies. These must all be formally documented in the corporate minutes.

Limitation on losses—Losses can only be deducted up to the amount of the shareholder's basis in the stock.

Basis in the stock is calculated as
Cash initially paid for stock
+ Cash contributed after initial investment
+ Value of property contributed for stock
+ Income that was taxed to you in the past, not received/distributed
- Dividends Received
- Losses passed through to you
Adjusted Basis of Stock

"Pass-through" of earnings—Because an S Corporation is a "pass-through" entity, capital cannot be accumulated at lower corporate tax rates within the corporation, as can be done with a C Corporation.

Phantom income—The pro rata share of S Corporation income is taxed to shareholders whether or not they received the cash. At a minimum, shareholder distributions should be made to the shareholders to cover the tax paid on behalf of the S Corporation.

Less ability to raise capital—Because of the limitation on the number of shareholders allowed, an S Corporation is limited to whatever assets the allowed shareholders can contribute.

Limitations on fringe benefits—Generally, fringe benefits such as health insurance are includable in the wages of the shareholders, rather than being treated as a business expense.

Distributions of profit—Distributions of profit must be made in the same proportion as ownership interest. No other type of allocation is permitted.

Who Should Operate as an S Corporation?

Businesses that are looking for limited liability protection.

Businesses that can afford the cost of incorporating and the ongoing cost of accounting and the cost of maintaining corporate documents.

Businesses that wish to take advantage of the 20% Qualified Business Income Exclusion.

Businesses that will be generating losses at the corporate level. These losses can be used by shareholders to reduce other income on their personal tax return. Deductible losses are limited to the shareholder's basis in the stock.

Businesses that are concerned about the possibility of double taxation. There is no tax at the corporate level for S Corporations. All S Corporation income is taxed at the individual shareholder level. Thus, there is little need to monitor the income of the corporation at year-end to determine if it is necessary to pay additional salary or bonuses to the shareholders to reduce the Corporate Income Tax.

Businesses that wish to split income between family members in lower tax brackets. Having family members who are in lower tax brackets own shares in the corporation shifts income and lower taxes.

Who Should Not Operate as an S Corporation?

Businesses that have more than 100 shareholders, or that anticipate having more than 100 shareholders in the future should not consider forming an S Corporation due to the limitation on the number of shareholders.

Any business contemplating having shareholders consisting of either partnerships or other corporations. S Corporations cannot be owned by partnerships or other corporations.

Any business that has foreign shareholders. All shareholders of an S Corporation must be U.S. citizens.

Businesses that would like to accumulate capital within the corporation at lower tax rates. All income is taxed at the shareholders' tax rates which may be higher than the graduated rates of a C Corporation, regardless of whether or not cash is distributed.

Businesses that cannot afford the additional cost of incorporating the business, proper accounting, and the additional costs of maintaining the corporate documents.

Businesses that wish to allocate profit and losses in a

manner other than on a pro-rata basis. S Corporation profit and loss must be proportionately allocated in the same percentage as stock ownership.

Chapter 8

Limited Liability Company

What is a limited liability company? A limited liability company is a hybrid entity. A formal entity, organized and registered with the Secretary of State, an LLC has the limited liability protection provided by a corporation and is generally taxed like a partnership or sole proprietor, by default.

Ownership. A limited liability company can be owned by one or more persons. There is no limit on the number of persons that can be owners of a limited liability company.

If only one person owns the business, it is known as a single member LLC. If there is more than one owner is it known as a multiple member LLC.

An LLC can be member-managed, or managed by a manager.

Ease of formation. The LLC must register "Articles of Organization" with the Secretary of State. Other than tax reporting, there are no further documents that need to be maintained, unlike the requirements for a corporation.

It is generally a good idea to register your business name with your local authority to ensure no one else is using the name and to reserve your right to use the selected name.

It is also suggested that a formal LLC operating agreement be adopted and signed by all of the LLC members.

Items that should be included:

- Listing of duties and responsibilities of the members
- How the management of the LLC will be handled
- How changes to the LLC ownership will be handled upon the death, disability, retirement or withdrawal of a member
- Requirements for the admission of new members
- How income/losses will be allocated
- How and when member distributions will be made and how they will be determined
- What the capital contributions of the member will be and how the member interests will be divided

LLCs are a formal legally recognized entity. A limited liability company is a formal legal entity whose status is granted by the state in which it is organized.

Legal liability
The members of a limited liability company enjoy limited liability protection from the debts and other obligations of the business. This is generally considered to be one of the main advantages in the forming of an LLC.

It is suggested that an LLC maintain a business checking account, separate and distinct from the personal checking accounts of the members.

Tax reporting

LLCs are unique in that they can elect their tax treatment and even change how they are taxed as their businesses evolve.

The default treatment of a single member LLC is to be taxed like a sole proprietor. All business activity is reported on Schedule C of the LLC member's personal tax return.

The default treatment of a multiple member LLC is to be treated like a general partnership. All business activity is reported on Form 1065, "U. S. Return of Partnership Income."

If however, the LLC member(s) decide that the default treatment does not meet their needs, they can make an Entity Classification Election using Form 8832, and select the taxation structure that meets their needs.

The LLC may choose to be taxed as a C Corporation or an S Corporation. If it elects to be taxed as a particular entity, it must report their activities on the corresponding form. C Corporations must use a Form 1120, "U.S. Corporation Income Tax Return." S Corporations must use a Form 1120S, "U.S. Income Tax Return for an S Corporation."

Careful consideration must be made before making an election. While an entity election may be changed, that change is irreversible for five years.

Pass-through entity

LLCs **ARE** a Pass-Through entity, subject to the 20% Qualified Business Income Exclusion. Certain limitations may apply based upon type of business, taxable income, filing status, personal salary and assets employed in the business.

How is income allocated?

How income is allocated depends upon the number of members and any elections made.

For a single member LLC, all of the income belongs to the single member.

For a multiple member LLC, net income is allocated by default on a pro-rata basis among the members.

However, a limited liability company, absent an entity election is flexible in how income can be allocated to the members. Income and losses are not required to be allocated based upon the percentage ownership of the members and can be allocated to members in any manner in which they agree.

For example, all of the losses can be allocated to one member and all of the profits can be allocated to another member. Or an allocation can be made on a 75/25 % basis, when, in fact, there are only two members who each own 50%. The only requirement is that the entire amount of income or loss be allocated to someone.

Tax paying

How income is paid depends upon the number of members and any elections made.

For a single member LLC, all of the tax on the LLC income is paid by the single member.

For a multiple member LLC, income is allocated to each individual member, who must report and pay taxes on their pro-rata portion of the income or loss on their personal tax returns.

What taxes are involved?

The member's reported net income is subject to federal income tax. For a single member LLC, the income of the business is considered self-employment income, and is subject to self-employment tax. Self-employment tax is analogous to Social Security and Medicare taxes that are paid by employees.

For multiple member LLCs, the managing member's income of the business is considered self-employment income, subject to both federal income tax and self-employment tax.

Members who have non-managing status are subject to federal income tax but may not be subject to self-employment tax, if it's a manager-managed LLC.

How are the members paid?

A member can receive two types of income from a limited liability company. Members can receive guaranteed payments to partners for services performed, if those members are actively involved in the business.

Guaranteed payments to members are an expense of the LLC and reduce the net income of the LLC, and therefore the amount of income reported to the members. Guaranteed payments are reported on the appropriate member's Schedule K-1.

Member distributions are usually considered to be a distribution of income, similar to owner draws for a sole proprietor.

Members can have distributions made in any amount deemed appropriate by the members. They do not have to be made in accordance with percentage of ownership.

Member distributions are not considered income to the shareholder and are not subject to self-employment tax.

Member distributions that are made in excess of the balance in their capital account would be reported as income.

Advantages of a Limited Liability Company

Limited liability—LLCs generally have the same limited liability protection as corporations. The liability of members is limited to their investment in the LLC, plus any debts personally guaranteed.

Pass-through entity—LLCs ARE a Pass-Through entity, subject to the 20% Qualified Business Income Exclusion. Certain limitations may apply based upon type of business, taxable income, filing status, personal salary and assets employed in the business.

Relatively easy to set up—A limited liability company must file Articles of Organization with the Secretary of State. No other formal organization or legal paperwork is required, such as holding annual shareholder meetings or keeping of corporate minutes, as is required with corporations.

A newly formed limited liability company must obtain an Employer Identification Number (EIN) by completing Form SS-4, "Application for Employer Identification Number." This identifying number will be used by the LLC in all of its tax filings.

Flexibility in how the entity will be taxed—An LLC can change how it chooses to be taxed, as its needs change, by completing a Form 8832, "Entity Classification Election." This can only be done once every five years.

Multiple owners—A limited liability company may have one or more members (owners). An LLC operating with a single member would generally be taxed as a sole proprietor. An LLC with multiple members is generally taxed as a partnership.

There can be an unlimited number of partners in a limited liability company, unless a multiple member LLC chooses to be taxed as an S Corporation.

Easier to raise capital—Allowing multiple members to contribute capital to the business and having the ability to borrow money on behalf of the business, and not relying on a single or small number of members' personal credit, increases the capital raising ability of the entity.

More depth of management—Having more than one owner diversifies the management available to the business. The more members involved, the more talent, experience, and skill-sets are available to help grow and run the business.

Simplified payroll—There is no requirement to set up the members as employees and write payroll checks, or handle other responsibilities of having employees such as quarterly payroll tax filings, paying employment taxes and preparing an annual W-2.

If the LLC hires employees, then the entity must comply with all recordkeeping and filing requirements for their employees.

"Pass-through" of losses—Losses "pass through" to the member's personal tax return. These losses can be used to offset other taxable income of the members. This can be important if the LLC generates losses at the beginning of the business.

Deductibility of health insurance premiums—The managing members may deduct up to 100% of health insurance premiums for themselves and their family, limited to the extent of profit reported by the member. Non-managing members are unable to deduct health insurance premiums.

If the member is treated as being self-employed, health insurance premiums do not reduce the LLC's income, but the member can deduct the health insurance premium as an adjustment to income on their personal tax return.

Continuity of life—The death or resignation of a member will not end the life of the LLC. The remaining members can continue operating the business.

No double taxation of profits—All profits flow through to the members who pay tax on their personal tax returns. There is no income tax paid by the LLC such as would be paid by a C Corporation, if the LLC has accepted the default tax treatment or if they've elected to be taxed as an S Corporation, both of which are "pass-through" treatments (which means there is no "double taxation").

Disadvantages of a Limited Liability Company

More management—Although many people may consider having more partners/members and the additional talent that goes along with more partners as an asset, this may not always be the case.

Human nature will always come into play. Sometimes disagreements will arise concerning business decisions that can be tough to settle.

Complaints about money and draws—There can be major disagreements between the members concerning money. This can be the single largest problem faced by limited liability companies. More LLCs break up over money than any other reason.

Reasons for disagreements can include uneven distributions of profit based upon capital contributed, effort expended or results achieved. For example, two members may put equal time into the business but one may bring in 90% of the sales and the other only 10%. The fellow who brings in

90% of the clients may begin to feel taken advantage of. It's human nature.

A well-drafted LLC agreement should thoroughly address how member distributions should be handled.

Taxed on income—Members are personally responsible for the tax due on their pro-rata profits of the business, regardless of whether profits or money were taken from the business.

However, it is quite common for the LLC to make distributions to the members (which are not considered income) to cover the tax liability incurred by the members as a result of LLC income.

Difficulty raising capital—It can be much tougher raising capital as an LLC. The assets of the members and the LLC serve as the primary collateral for loans, which may not be enough for some lenders.

Who is a Limited Liability Company Best Suited For?

A limited liability company should be considered by businesses who wish to limit their exposure to liability.

Businesses that wish to take advantage of the 20% Qualified Business Income Exclusion.

A limited liability company should be considered by individuals with businesses that are just commencing operations. LLCs offer new businesses with much flexibility.

Many new businesses are not profitable in the first year or two and generate losses. Losses generated by the LLC can be used by the members to reduce their taxable income from other sources of income such as a working spouse, rental properties or investment income.

Limited liability companies have flexibility in ownership. An LLC can have as many owners as desired (assuming an S Corporation election has not been made).

The only expense of formation is organizing with the Secretary of State. No other formal documentation is required, other than a formal accounting for business and tax purposes.

Who Should Not Operate as a Limited Liability Company

Businesses that are not concerned with any potential liability exposure. This is one of the main non-tax features of an LLC. If you don't require limited liability, you can save money on organization costs by not forming an LLC.

Business with multiple members who are not familiar with one another. It is suggested that you know your member/partner very well before going into business with them. Working closely together is like being married – and you want make sure you know your partner very well before embarking on such a venture.

Ideally, partners/members should bring different sets of skills to the business, such as having one member exceptionally talented in marketing, and another member/partner with complementary skills such as finance or operations.

An age-old saying, "Two heads are better than one" can be very helpful in a small business partnership.

Final Thoughts

I trust you found the information in this book helpful.

My goal in sharing it with you was to give you the basic information needed to help you select the appropriate entity for your business so that you can accomplish your non-tax objectives and at the same time legally minimize the taxes that you pay.

I hope you now better understand the many choices available to you in selecting an entity that will best accomplish your business and tax needs.

As you have seen, when evaluating which form of business will best suit your tax and non-tax business needs, there is not a one-size-fits-all single best answer.

There are many factors that must be evaluated, taking into account your personal situation.

Now you must take the next step.

I understand that making changes in life can be scary, and

not something that you may look forward to doing without at least a little apprehension. However, starting a business can be an extremely rewarding experience.

In many cases, a business is the single largest investment that a person makes. How you choose to structure and operate your business will ultimately determine how much the business will benefit you, the lifestyle you're going to lead, how you're going to educate your children, how you're going to retire, and how much money you get to keep and put in your pockets.

But I promise you, after you adopt the appropriate entity for your business and begin to reap the benefits of lower taxes, the time spent analyzing entities will have been worth it.

The Types of Clients That I Accept

I am very selective about the kinds of clients that I accept into my practice.

The first criteria I am looking for is an individual who owns either a new or existing business. Many but not all of the tax strategies that I suggest and employ are only available to taxpayers who own their own businesses.

This taxpayer must be the main decision maker. If a taxpayer has no ability to make the final decision to implement a particular strategy, all the tax planning strategies that I suggest will be useless. Implementation is critical.

The taxpayer must be open to new ideas and willing to change. If a taxpayer doesn't want to change anything in the way that they structure their affairs, then nothing will change in their situation and the taxes that they pay.

The taxpayer must be honest and ethical and willing to work within the rules and regulations of the IRS. Clients interested in intentionally understating income or overstating expenses are committing fraud, and I will not knowingly become involved with these types of taxpayers.

The Types of Clients That I Don't Accept

I enjoy I enjoy working with taxpayers to help them minimize their taxes through tax planning.

However, if a taxpayer is an employee and not a business owner, the options available to us for serious tax planning are limited.

If a taxpayer wants to continue doing things the way they have always done them, and not be open to change, they will not benefit from a tax planning engagement with me.

Clients who are interested in filing fraudulent tax returns don't need tax planning. The IRS statute of limitations for FRAUD is unlimited—the IRS has forever to audit any returns that they suspect are fraudulent. And, "forever" is a very long time.

So if any of these above situations describes you, please don't call. My practice is not set up to help you!

Glossary of Terms

Accelerated Depreciation A method of recording depreciation faster than with straight line depreciation. More depreciation is recorded in the earlier years than in the later years.

Accrual Basis The method of accounting that looks at whether income has been earned (whether or not received), and whether an expense has been incurred (whether or not paid).

Buy-Sell Agreement An agreement detailing the future buyout of partners or owners.

C Corporation A corporation that chooses to be taxed at the corporate level.

Capital An account that tracks an owner's or partner's interest in the business.

Cash Basis The method of accounting that records income when actually received, and expenses when actually paid.

DBA "Doing Business As" The registering of your business name with the local city or state authorities. Also known as a fictitious name.

Double Taxation Describes the situation where an entity pays tax once at the corporate level, and the income is taxed a second time when it is paid to the taxpayer.

Effective Tax Rate Total tax paid divided by total income.

Estimated Tax Payment A quarterly tax payment made during the year for estimated annual tax liability.

Form 1040 The form used to file an individual's personal tax return.

Form 1065 The form used to file a partnership tax return.

Form 1120 The form used to file a C Corporation tax return.

Form 1120S The form used to file an S Corporation tax return.

Form 2553 The election form used to request S Corporation status.

Form 8823 The election form used to select the desired method of taxation when forming an LLC.

General Partner An owner of a general partnership, or the managing partner in a limited partnership.

General Partnership An unincorporated business operated by two or more individuals.

Limited Liability Company An entity owned by one or more owners in which the owners have limited liability.

Limited Partnership A partnership in which the limited partners have limited liability. One or more general partners have unlimited liabilities.

Marginal Tax Rate The tax rate that applies to the next dollar a taxpayer earns.

Member An owner of a limited liability company (LLC).

Multiple member LLC An LLC that has more than one owner/member.

Owner Draw Profit distribution taken by a sole proprietorship from their business.

Partner An owner of a partnership.

Partnership distribution Money paid from a partnership to a partner.

Pass-through entity An entity that reports their taxes, but doesn't pay their taxes. Income or loss is "passed through" to the owners of the business who pay the tax.

Qualified Business Exclusion Pass-through entities are eligible for the 20% Qualified Business Income Exclusion. Certain limitations may apply based upon type of business, taxable income, filing status, personal salary and assets employed in the business.

S Corporation Distribution Money paid from an S Corporation to a shareholder.

Schedule C Form used to report income and expenses of a sole proprietorship.

Self employment tax Tax paid on the earnings of a self-employed individual. Similar to the Social Security and Medicare tax.

Shareholder An owner of a corporation.

Single Member LLC A limited liability company with only one member/owner, as opposed to multiple member/owners. Treated as a sole proprietor for tax purposes.

Sole Proprietorship An unincorporated business operated by a single individual.

Tax Credit An item on a personal tax returns that reduces the tax owed dollar for dollar ($1 dollar tax credit equals $1 dollar of tax savings).

Tax Deduction An expense item on the tax return that reduces taxable income dollar for dollar. Tax reductions reduce tax by the amount of the marginal tax bracket.

Tax Savings A reduction in tax that would otherwise have been paid before tax planning.

Taxable Income The net income amount subject to federal income tax. Represents total income less adjustments less itemized or standard deduction and less personal exemptions.

Frequently Used Forms

Form SS-4
Application for Employer Identification Number
Page 1

Form **SS-4** (Rev. January 2010) Department of the Treasury Internal Revenue Service

Application for Employer Identification Number

(For use by employers, corporations, partnerships, trusts, estates, churches, government agencies, Indian tribal entities, certain individuals, and others.)

▶ See separate instructions for each line. ▶ Keep a copy for your records.

OMB No. 1545-0003

EIN

Type or print clearly.

1 Legal name of entity (or individual) for whom the EIN is being requested

2 Trade name of business (if different from name on line 1)

3 Executor, administrator, trustee, "care of" name

4a Mailing address (room, apt., suite no. and street, or P.O. box)

5a Street address (if different) (Do not enter a P.O. box.)

4b City, state, and ZIP code (if foreign, see instructions)

5b City, state, and ZIP code (if foreign, see instructions)

6 County and state where principal business is located

7a Name of responsible party

7b SSN, ITIN, or EIN

8a Is this application for a limited liability company (LLC) (or a foreign equivalent)? ☐ Yes ☐ No

8b If 8a is "Yes," enter the number of LLC members ▶

8c If 8a is "Yes," was the LLC organized in the United States? ☐ Yes ☐ No

9a **Type of entity** (check only one box). **Caution.** If 8a is "Yes," see the instructions for the correct box to check.

- ☐ Sole proprietor (SSN)
- ☐ Partnership
- ☐ Corporation (enter form number to be filed) ▶
- ☐ Personal service corporation
- ☐ Church or church-controlled organization
- ☐ Other nonprofit organization (specify) ▶
- ☐ Other (specify) ▶
- ☐ Estate (SSN of decedent)
- ☐ Plan administrator (TIN)
- ☐ Trust (TIN of grantor)
- ☐ National Guard
- ☐ Farmers' cooperative
- ☐ REMIC
- ☐ State/local government
- ☐ Federal government/military
- ☐ Indian tribal governments/enterprises

Group Exemption Number (GEN) if any ▶

9b If a corporation, name the state or foreign country (if applicable) where incorporated — State — Foreign country

10 **Reason for applying** (check only one box)

- ☐ Started new business (specify type) ▶
- ☐ Hired employees (Check the box and see line 13.)
- ☐ Compliance with IRS withholding regulations
- ☐ Other (specify) ▶
- ☐ Banking purpose (specify purpose) ▶
- ☐ Changed type of organization (specify new type) ▶
- ☐ Purchased going business
- ☐ Created a trust (specify type) ▶
- ☐ Created a pension plan (specify type) ▶

11 Date business started or acquired (month, day, year). See instructions.

12 Closing month of accounting year

13 Highest number of employees expected in the next 12 months (enter -0- if none). If no employees expected, skip line 14.

Agricultural	Household	Other

14 If you expect your employment tax liability to be $1,000 or less in a full calendar year and want to file Form 944 annually instead of Forms 941 quarterly, check here. (Your employment tax liability generally will be $1,000 or less if you expect to pay $4,000 or less in total wages.) If you do not check this box, you must file Form 941 for every quarter. ☐

15 First date wages or annuities were paid (month, day, year). **Note.** If applicant is a withholding agent, enter date income will first be paid to nonresident alien (month, day, year) ▶

16 Check **one** box that best describes the principal activity of your business

- ☐ Health care & social assistance
- ☐ Wholesale-agent/broker
- ☐ Construction
- ☐ Rental & leasing
- ☐ Transportation & warehousing
- ☐ Accommodation & food service
- ☐ Wholesale-other
- ☐ Retail
- ☐ Real estate
- ☐ Manufacturing
- ☐ Finance & insurance
- ☐ Other (specify) ▶

17 Indicate principal line of merchandise sold, specific construction work done, products produced, or services provided.

18 Has the applicant entity shown on line 1 ever applied for and received an EIN? ☐ Yes ☐ No

If "Yes," write previous EIN here ▶

Third Party Designee

Complete this section **only** if you want to authorize the named individual to receive the entity's EIN and answer questions about the completion of this form.

Designee's name — Designee's telephone number (include area code)

Address and ZIP code — Designee's fax number (include area code)

Under penalties of perjury, I declare that I have examined this application, and to the best of my knowledge and belief, it is true, correct, and complete.

Applicant's telephone number (include area code)

Name and title (type or print clearly) ▶

Applicant's fax number (include area code)

Signature ▶ Date ▶

For Privacy Act and Paperwork Reduction Act Notice, see separate instructions. Cat. No. 16055N Form **SS-4** (Rev. 1-2010)

Form SS-4
Application for Employer Identification Number
Page 2

Form SS-4 (Rev. 1-2010) Page 2

Do I Need an EIN?

File Form SS-4 if the applicant entity does not already have an EIN but is required to show an EIN on any return, statement, or other document.[1] See also the separate instructions for each line on Form SS-4.

IF the applicant...	AND...	THEN...
Started a new business	Does not currently have (nor expect to have) employees	Complete lines 1, 2, 4a–8a, 8b–c (if applicable), 9a, 9b (if applicable), and 10–14 and 16–18.
Hired (or will hire) employees, including household employees	Does not already have an EIN	Complete lines 1, 2, 4a–6, 7a–b (if applicable), 8a, 8b–c (if applicable), 9a, 9b (if applicable), 10–18.
Opened a bank account	Needs an EIN for banking purposes only	Complete lines 1–5b, 7a–b (if applicable), 8a, 8b–c (if applicable), 9a, 9b (if applicable), 10, and 18.
Changed type of organization	Either the legal character of the organization or its ownership changed (for example, you incorporate a sole proprietorship or form a partnership)[2]	Complete lines 1–18 (as applicable).
Purchased a going business[3]	Does not already have an EIN	Complete lines 1–18 (as applicable).
Created a trust	The trust is other than a grantor trust or an IRA trust[4]	Complete lines 1–18 (as applicable).
Created a pension plan as a plan administrator[5]	Needs an EIN for reporting purposes	Complete lines 1, 3, 4a–5b, 9a, 10, and 18.
Is a foreign person needing an EIN to comply with IRS withholding regulations	Needs an EIN to complete a Form W-8 (other than Form W-8ECI), avoid withholding on portfolio assets, or claim tax treaty benefits[6]	Complete lines 1–5b, 7a–b (SSN or ITIN optional), 8a, 8b–c (if applicable), 9a, 9b (if applicable), 10, and 18.
Is administering an estate	Needs an EIN to report estate income on Form 1041	Complete lines 1–6, 9a, 10–12, 13–17 (if applicable), and 18.
Is a withholding agent for taxes on non-wage income paid to an alien (i.e., individual, corporation, or partnership, etc.)	Is an agent, broker, fiduciary, manager, tenant, or spouse who is required to file Form 1042, Annual Withholding Tax Return for U.S. Source Income of Foreign Persons	Complete lines 1, 2, 3 (if applicable), 4a–5b, 7a–b (if applicable), 8a, 8b–c (if applicable), 9a, 9b (if applicable), 10, and 18.
Is a state or local agency	Serves as a tax reporting agent for public assistance recipients under Rev. Proc. 80-4, 1980-1 C.B. 581[7]	Complete lines 1, 2, 4a–5b, 9a, 10, and 18.
Is a single-member LLC	Needs an EIN to file Form 8832, Classification Election, for filing employment tax returns and excise tax returns, or for state reporting purposes[8]	Complete lines 1–18 (as applicable).
Is an S corporation	Needs an EIN to file Form 2553, Election by a Small Business Corporation[9]	Complete lines 1–18 (as applicable).

[1] For example, a sole proprietorship or self-employed farmer who establishes a qualified retirement plan, or is required to file excise, employment, alcohol, tobacco, or firearms returns, must have an EIN. A partnership, corporation, REMIC (real estate mortgage investment conduit), nonprofit organization (church, club, etc.), or farmers' cooperative must use an EIN for any tax-related purpose even if the entity does not have employees.

[2] However, do not apply for a new EIN if the existing entity only (a) changed its business name, (b) elected on Form 8832 to change the way it is taxed (or is covered by the default rules), or (c) terminated its partnership status because at least 50% of the total interests in partnership capital and profits were sold or exchanged within a 12-month period. The EIN of the terminated partnership should continue to be used. See Regulations section 301.6109-1(d)(2)(iii).

[3] Do not use the EIN of the prior business unless you became the "owner" of a corporation by acquiring its stock.

[4] However, grantor trusts that do not file using Optional Method 1 and IRA trusts that are required to file Form 990-T, Exempt Organization Business Income Tax Return, must have an EIN. For more information on grantor trusts, see the Instructions for Form 1041.

[5] A plan administrator is the person or group of persons specified as the administrator by the instrument under which the plan is operated.

[6] Entities applying to be a Qualified Intermediary (QI) need a QI-EIN even if they already have an EIN. See Rev. Proc. 2000-12.

[7] See also *Household employer* on page 4 of the instructions. **Note.** State or local agencies may need an EIN for other reasons, for example, hired employees.

[8] See *Disregarded entities* on page 4 of the instructions for details on completing Form SS-4 for an LLC.

[9] An existing corporation that is electing or revoking S corporation status should use its previously assigned EIN.

Form 8832
Entity Classification Election
Page 1

Form **8832** (Rev. December 2013)
Department of the Treasury
Internal Revenue Service

Entity Classification Election

► **Information about Form 8832 and its instructions is at** ***www.irs.gov/form8832.***

OMB No. 1545-1516

Type or Print

Name of eligible entity making election | **Employer identification number**

Number, street, and room or suite no. If a P.O. box, see instructions.

City or town, state, and ZIP code. If a foreign address, enter city, province or state, postal code and country. Follow the country's practice for entering the postal code.

► Check if ☐ Address change ☐ Late classification relief sought under Revenue Procedure 2009-41
☐ Relief for a late change of entity classification election sought under Revenue Procedure 2010-32

Part I **Election Information**

1 **Type of election** (see instructions):

a ☐ Initial classification by a newly-formed entity. Skip lines 2a and 2b and go to line 3.
b ☐ Change in current classification. Go to line 2a.

2a Has the eligible entity previously filed an entity election that had an effective date within the last 60 months?

☐ **Yes.** Go to line 2b.
☐ **No.** Skip line 2b and go to line 3.

2b Was the eligible entity's prior election an initial classification election by a newly formed entity that was effective on the date of formation?

☐ **Yes.** Go to line 3.
☐ **No.** Stop here. You generally are not currently eligible to make the election (see instructions).

3 Does the eligible entity have more than one owner?

☐ **Yes.** You can elect to be classified as a partnership or an association taxable as a corporation. Skip line 4 and go to line 5.
☐ **No.** You can elect to be classified as an association taxable as a corporation or to be disregarded as a separate entity. Go to line 4.

4 If the eligible entity has only one owner, provide the following information:

a Name of owner ► ....
b Identifying number of owner ► ....

5 If the eligible entity is owned by one or more affiliated corporations that file a consolidated return, provide the name and employer identification number of the parent corporation:

a Name of parent corporation ► ....
b Employer identification number ► ....

For Paperwork Reduction Act Notice, see instructions. Cat. No. 22598R Form **8832** (Rev. 12-2013)

Form 8832
Entity Classification Election
Page 2

Form 8832 (Rev. 12-2013) Page **2**

Part I **Election Information** (Continued)

6 **Type of entity** (see instructions):

- **a** ☐ A domestic eligible entity electing to be classified as an association taxable as a corporation.
- **b** ☐ A domestic eligible entity electing to be classified as a partnership.
- **c** ☐ A domestic eligible entity with a single owner electing to be disregarded as a separate entity.
- **d** ☐ A foreign eligible entity electing to be classified as an association taxable as a corporation.
- **e** ☐ A foreign eligible entity electing to be classified as a partnership.
- **f** ☐ A foreign eligible entity with a single owner electing to be disregarded as a separate entity.

7 If the eligible entity is created or organized in a foreign jurisdiction, provide the foreign country of organization ▶

8 Election is to be effective beginning (month, day, year) (see instructions) . . . . ▶

9 Name and title of contact person whom the IRS may call for more information | **10** Contact person's telephone number

Consent Statement and Signature(s) (see instructions)

Under penalties of perjury, I (we) declare that I (we) consent to the election of the above-named entity to be classified as indicated above, and that I (we) have examined this election and consent statement, and to the best of my (our) knowledge and belief, this election and consent statement are true, correct, and complete. If I am an officer, manager, or member signing for the entity, I further declare under penalties of perjury that I am authorized to make the election on its behalf.

Signature(s)	Date	Title

Form **8832** (Rev. 12-2013)

Form 2553
Election by a Small Business Corporation
Page 1
S Corporation Election

Form **2553**
(Rev. December 2013)
Department of the Treasury
Internal Revenue Service

Election by a Small Business Corporation
(Under section 1362 of the Internal Revenue Code)
▶ See Parts II and III on page 3.
▶ You can fax this form to the IRS (see separate instructions).
▶ Information about Form 2553 and its separate instructions is at *www.irs.gov/form2553.*

OMB No. 1545-0123

Note. This election to be an S corporation can be accepted only if all the tests are met under *Who May Elect* in the instructions, all shareholders have signed the consent statement, an officer has signed below, and the exact name and address of the corporation (entity) and other required form information have been provided.

Part I **Election Information**

Type or Print

Name (see instructions) | **A** Employer identification number
Number, street, and room or suite no. (If a P.O. box, see instructions.) | **B** Date incorporated
City or town, state, and ZIP code | **C** State of incorporation

D Check the applicable box(es) if the corporation (entity), after applying for the EIN shown in **A** above, changed its ☐ name or ☐ address

E Election is to be effective for tax year beginning (month, day, year) (see instructions) ▶
Caution. A corporation (entity) making the election for its first tax year in existence will usually enter the beginning date of a short tax year that begins on a date other than January 1.

F Selected tax year:
(1) ☐ Calendar year
(2) ☐ Fiscal year ending (month and day) ▶
(3) ☐ 52-53-week year ending with reference to the month of December
(4) ☐ 52-53-week year ending with reference to the month of ▶
If box (2) or (4) is checked, complete Part II.

G If more than 100 shareholders are listed for item J (see page 2), check this box if treating members of a family as one shareholder results in no more than 100 shareholders (see test 2 under *Who May Elect* in the instructions) ▶ ☐

H Name and title of officer or legal representative who the IRS may call for more information | **I** Telephone number of officer or legal representative

If this S corporation election is being filed late, I declare that I had reasonable cause for not filing Form 2553 timely, and if this late election is being made by an entity eligible to elect to be treated as a corporation, I declare that I also had reasonable cause for not filing an entity classification election timely and that the representations listed in Part IV are true. See below for my explanation of the reasons the election or elections were not made on time and a description of my diligent actions to correct the mistake upon its discovery (see instructions).

Sign Here
Under penalties of perjury, I declare that I have examined this election, including accompanying documents, and, to the best of my knowledge and belief, the election contains all the relevant facts relating to the election, and such facts are true, correct, and complete.

▶ **Signature of officer** | **Title** | **Date**

For Paperwork Reduction Act Notice, see separate instructions. Cat. No. 18629R Form **2553** (Rev. 12-2013)

Form 2553
Election by a Small Business Corporation
Page 2
S Corportation Election

Form 2553 (Rev. 12-2013) Page **2**

Part I **Election Information** (continued) **Note.** If you need more rows, use additional copies of page 2.

J Name and address of each shareholder or former shareholder required to consent to the election (see instructions)	K **Shareholder's Consent Statement** Under penalties of perjury, I declare that I consent to the election of the above-named corporation (entity) to be an S corporation under section 1362(a) and that I have examined this consent statement, including accompanying documents, and, to the best of my knowledge and belief, the election contains all the relevant facts relating to the election, and such facts are true, correct, and complete. I understand my consent is binding and may not be withdrawn after the corporation (entity) has made a valid election. If seeking relief for a late filed election, I also declare under penalties of perjury that I have reported my income on all affected returns consistent with the S corporation election for the year for which the election should have been filed (see beginning date entered on line E) and for all subsequent years.		L Stock owned or percentage of ownership (see instructions)		M Social security number or employer identification number (see instructions)	N Shareholder's tax year ends (month and day)
	Signature	Date	Number of shares or percentage of ownership	Date(s) acquired		

Form **2553** (Rev. 12-2013)

Form 2553
Election by a Small Business Corporation
Page 3
S Corportation Election

Form 2553 (Rev. 12-2013) Page 3

Part II Selection of Fiscal Tax Year (see instructions)

Note. All corporations using this part must complete item O and item P, Q, or R.

O Check the applicable box to indicate whether the corporation is:

1. ☐ A new corporation **adopting** the tax year entered in item F, Part I.
2. ☐ An existing corporation **retaining** the tax year entered in item F, Part I.
3. ☐ An existing corporation **changing** to the tax year entered in item F, Part I.

P Complete item P if the corporation is using the automatic approval provisions of Rev. Proc. 2006-46, 2006-45 I.R.B. 859, to request (1) a natural business year (as defined in section 5.07 of Rev. Proc. 2006-46) or (2) a year that satisfies the ownership tax year test (as defined in section 5.08 of Rev. Proc. 2006-46). Check the applicable box below to indicate the representation statement the corporation is making.

1. Natural Business Year ▶ ☐ I represent that the corporation is adopting, retaining, or changing to a tax year that qualifies as its natural business year (as defined in section 5.07 of Rev. Proc. 2006-46) and has attached a statement showing separately for each month the gross receipts for the most recent 47 months (see instructions). I also represent that the corporation is not precluded by section 4.02 of Rev. Proc. 2006-46 from obtaining automatic approval of such adoption, retention, or change in tax year.

2. Ownership Tax Year ▶ ☐ I represent that shareholders (as described in section 5.08 of Rev. Proc. 2006-46) holding more than half of the shares of the stock (as of the first day of the tax year to which the request relates) of the corporation have the same tax year or are concurrently changing to the tax year that the corporation adopts, retains, or changes to per item F, Part I, and that such tax year satisfies the requirement of section 4.01(3) of Rev. Proc. 2006-46. I also represent that the corporation is not precluded by section 4.02 of Rev. Proc. 2006-46 from obtaining automatic approval of such adoption, retention, or change in tax year.

Note. If you do not use item P and the corporation wants a fiscal tax year, complete either item Q or R below. Item Q is used to request a fiscal tax year based on a business purpose and to make a back-up section 444 election. Item R is used to make a regular section 444 election.

Q Business Purpose—To request a fiscal tax year based on a business purpose, check box Q1. See instructions for details including payment of a user fee. You may also check box Q2 and/or box Q3.

1. Check here ▶ ☐ if the fiscal year entered in item F, Part I, is requested under the prior approval provisions of Rev. Proc. 2002-39, 2002-22 I.R.B. 1046. Attach to Form 2553 a statement describing the relevant facts and circumstances and, if applicable, the gross receipts from sales and services necessary to establish a business purpose. See the instructions for details regarding the gross receipts from sales and services. If the IRS proposes to disapprove the requested fiscal year, do you want a conference with the IRS National Office?

☐ Yes ☐ No

2. Check here ▶ ☐ to show that the corporation intends to make a back-up section 444 election in the event the corporation's business purpose request is not approved by the IRS. (See instructions for more information.)

3. Check here ▶ ☐ to show that the corporation agrees to adopt or change to a tax year ending December 31 if necessary for the IRS to accept this election for S corporation status in the event (1) the corporation's business purpose request is not approved and the corporation makes a back-up section 444 election, but is ultimately not qualified to make a section 444 election, or (2) the corporation's business purpose request is not approved and the corporation did not make a back-up section 444 election.

R Section 444 Election—To make a section 444 election, check box R1. You may also check box R2.

1. Check here ▶ ☐ to show that the corporation will make, if qualified, a section 444 election to have the fiscal tax year shown in item F, Part I. To make the election, you must complete **Form 8716**, Election To Have a Tax Year Other Than a Required Tax Year, and either attach it to Form 2553 or file it separately.

2. Check here ▶ ☐ to show that the corporation agrees to adopt or change to a tax year ending December 31 if necessary for the IRS to accept this election for S corporation status in the event the corporation is ultimately not qualified to make a section 444 election.

Part III Qualified Subchapter S Trust (QSST) Election Under Section 1361(d)(2)*

Income beneficiary's name and address	Social security number
Trust's name and address	Employer identification number

Date on which stock of the corporation was transferred to the trust (month, day, year) ▶

In order for the trust named above to be a QSST and thus a qualifying shareholder of the S corporation for which this Form 2553 is filed, I hereby make the election under section 1361(d)(2). Under penalties of perjury, I certify that the trust meets the definitional requirements of section 1361(d)(3) and that all other information provided in Part III is true, correct, and complete.

Signature of income beneficiary or signature and title of legal representative or other qualified person making the election Date

*Use Part III to make the QSST election only if stock of the corporation has been transferred to the trust on or before the date on which the corporation makes its election to be an S corporation. The QSST election must be made and filed separately if stock of the corporation is transferred to the trust **after** the date on which the corporation makes the S election.

Form **2553** (Rev. 12-2013)

Schedule C
Profit or Loss from Business
Page 1
Sole Proprietorship

SCHEDULE C (Form 1040)
Department of the Treasury
Internal Revenue Service (99)

Profit or Loss From Business
(Sole Proprietorship)

▶ **Information about Schedule C and its separate instructions is at** ***www.irs.gov/schedulec.***
▶ **Attach to Form 1040, 1040NR, or 1041; partnerships generally must file Form 1065.**

OMB No. 1545-0074
Attachment Sequence No. 09

Name of proprietor | **Social security number (SSN)**

A Principal business or profession, including product or service (see instructions) | **B Enter code from instructions** ▶

C Business name. If no separate business name, leave blank. | D Employer ID number (EIN), (see instr.)

E Business address (including suite or room no.) ▶
City, town or post office, state, and ZIP code

F Accounting method: (1) ☐ Cash (2) ☐ Accrual (3) ☐ Other (specify) ▶

G Did you "materially participate" in the operation of this business during 2016? If "No," see instructions for limit on losses ☐ **Yes** ☐ **No**

H If you started or acquired this business during 2016, check here ▶ ☐

I Did you make any payments in 2016 that would require you to file Form(s) 1099? (see instructions) ☐ **Yes** ☐ **No**

J If "Yes," did you or will you file required Forms 1099? ☐ **Yes** ☐ **No**

Part I Income

1	Gross receipts or sales. See instructions for line 1 and check the box if this income was reported to you on Form W-2 and the "Statutory employee" box on that form was checked ▶ ☐	1	
2	Returns and allowances	2	
3	Subtract line 2 from line 1	3	
4	Cost of goods sold (from line 42)	4	
5	**Gross profit.** Subtract line 4 from line 3	5	
6	Other income, including federal and state gasoline or fuel tax credit or refund (see instructions)	6	
7	**Gross income.** Add lines 5 and 6 ▶	7	

Part II Expenses. Enter expenses for business use of your home **only** on line 30.

8	Advertising	8		18	Office expense (see instructions)	18	
9	Car and truck expenses (see instructions)	9		19	Pension and profit-sharing plans	19	
				20	Rent or lease (see instructions):		
10	Commissions and fees	10		a	Vehicles, machinery, and equipment	20a	
11	Contract labor (see instructions)	11		b	Other business property	20b	
12	Depletion	12		21	Repairs and maintenance	21	
13	Depreciation and section 179 expense deduction (not included in Part III) (see instructions)	13		22	Supplies (not included in Part III)	22	
				23	Taxes and licenses	23	
				24	Travel, meals, and entertainment:		
14	Employee benefit programs (other than on line 19)	14		a	Travel	24a	
15	Insurance (other than health)	15		b	Deductible meals and entertainment (see instructions)	24b	
16	Interest:			25	Utilities	25	
a	Mortgage (paid to banks, etc.)	16a		26	Wages (less employment credits)	26	
b	Other	16b		27a	Other expenses (from line 48)	27a	
17	Legal and professional services	17		b	**Reserved for future use**	27b	

28	**Total expenses** before expenses for business use of home. Add lines 8 through 27a ▶	28	
29	Tentative profit or (loss). Subtract line 28 from line 7	29	
30	Expenses for business use of your home. Do not report these expenses elsewhere. Attach Form 8829 unless using the simplified method (see instructions). **Simplified method filers only:** enter the total square footage of: (a) your home ______ and (b) the part of your home used for business: ______. Use the Simplified Method Worksheet in the instructions to figure the amount to enter on line 30	30	
31	**Net profit or (loss).** Subtract line 30 from line 29. • If a profit, enter on both **Form 1040, line 12** (or **Form 1040NR, line** 13) and on **Schedule SE, line 2**. (If you checked the box on line 1, see instructions). Estates and trusts, enter on **Form 1041, line 3.** • If a loss, you **must** go to line 32.	31	

32 If you have a loss, check the box that describes your investment in this activity (see instructions).
• If you checked 32a, enter the loss on both **Form 1040, line 12,** (or **Form 1040NR, line 13**) and on **Schedule SE, line 2.** (If you checked the box on line 1, see the line 31 instructions). Estates and trusts, enter on **Form 1041, line 3.**
• If you checked 32b, you **must** attach **Form 6198.** Your loss may be limited.

32a ☐ All investment is at risk.
32b ☐ Some investment is not at risk.

For Paperwork Reduction Act Notice, see the separate instructions. Cat. No. 11334P **Schedule C (Form 1040) 2016**

Schedule C
Profit or Loss from Business
Page 2
Sole Proprietorship

Schedule C (Form 1040) 2016 Page **2**

Part III **Cost of Goods Sold** (see instructions)

33 Method(s) used to value closing inventory a ☐ Cost b ☐ Lower of cost or market c ☐ Other (attach explanation)

34 Was there any change in determining quantities, costs, or valuations between opening and closing inventory? If "Yes," attach explanation ☐ Yes ☐ No

35 Inventory at beginning of year. If different from last year's closing inventory, attach explanation . . . 35

36 Purchases less cost of items withdrawn for personal use . . . 36

37 Cost of labor. Do not include any amounts paid to yourself . . . 37

38 Materials and supplies . . . 38

39 Other costs . . . 39

40 Add lines 35 through 39 . . . 40

41 Inventory at end of year . . . 41

42 **Cost of goods sold.** Subtract line 41 from line 40. Enter the result here and on line 4 . . . 42

Part IV **Information on Your Vehicle.** Complete this part **only** if you are claiming car or truck expenses on line 9 and are not required to file Form 4562 for this business. See the instructions for line 13 to find out if you must file Form 4562.

43 When did you place your vehicle in service for business purposes? (month, day, year) ▶ / /

44 Of the total number of miles you drove your vehicle during 2016, enter the number of miles you used your vehicle for:

a Business b Commuting (see instructions) c Other

45 Was your vehicle available for personal use during off-duty hours? . . . ☐ Yes ☐ No

46 Do you (or your spouse) have another vehicle available for personal use? . . . ☐ Yes ☐ No

47a Do you have evidence to support your deduction? . . . ☐ Yes ☐ No

b If "Yes," is the evidence written? . . . ☐ Yes ☐ No

Part V **Other Expenses.** List below business expenses not included on lines 8–26 or line 30.

48 **Total other expenses.** Enter here and on line 27a . . . 48

Schedule C (Form 1040) 2016

Form 1065
Partnership Return
Page 1 Only

Form **1065** Department of the Treasury Internal Revenue Service

U.S. Return of Partnership Income

For calendar year 2016, or tax year beginning , 2016, ending , 20

▶ **Information about Form 1065 and its separate instructions is at *www.irs.gov/form1065*.**

OMB No. 1545-0123

A Principal business activity	Type or Print	Name of partnership	D Employer identification number
B Principal product or service		Number, street, and room or suite no. If a P.O. box, see the instructions.	E Date business started
C Business code number		City or town, state or province, country, and ZIP or foreign postal code	F Total assets (see the instructions) $

G Check applicable boxes: (1) ☐ Initial return (2) ☐ Final return (3) ☐ Name change (4) ☐ Address change (5) ☐ Amended return
(6) ☐ Technical termination - also check (1) or (2)

H Check accounting method (1) ☐ Cash (2) ☐ Accrual (3) ☐ Other (specify) ▶

I Number of Schedules K-1. Attach one for each person who was a partner at any time during the tax year ▶

J Check if Schedules C and M-3 are attached ☐

Caution. *Include **only** trade or business income and expenses on lines 1a through 22 below. See the instructions for more information.*

Income	1a	Gross receipts or sales	1a		
	b	Returns and allowances	1b		
	c	Balance. Subtract line 1b from line 1a		1c	
	2	Cost of goods sold (attach Form 1125-A)		2	
	3	Gross profit. Subtract line 2 from line 1c		3	
	4	Ordinary income (loss) from other partnerships, estates, and trusts (attach statement)		4	
	5	Net farm profit (loss) (attach Schedule F (Form 1040))		5	
	6	Net gain (loss) from Form 4797, Part II, line 17 (attach Form 4797)		6	
	7	Other income (loss) (attach statement)		7	
	8	**Total income (loss).** Combine lines 3 through 7		8	
Deductions (see the instructions for limitations)	9	Salaries and wages (other than to partners) (less employment credits)		9	
	10	Guaranteed payments to partners		10	
	11	Repairs and maintenance		11	
	12	Bad debts		12	
	13	Rent		13	
	14	Taxes and licenses		14	
	15	Interest		15	
	16a	Depreciation (if required, attach Form 4562)	16a		
	b	Less depreciation reported on Form 1125-A and elsewhere on return	16b	16c	
	17	Depletion **(Do not deduct oil and gas depletion.)**		17	
	18	Retirement plans, etc.		18	
	19	Employee benefit programs		19	
	20	Other deductions (attach statement)		20	
	21	**Total deductions.** Add the amounts shown in the far right column for lines 9 through 20.		21	
	22	**Ordinary business income (loss).** Subtract line 21 from line 8		22	

Sign Here

Under penalties of perjury, I declare that I have examined this return, including accompanying schedules and statements, and to the best of my knowledge and belief, it is true, correct, and complete. Declaration of preparer (other than general partner or limited liability company member manager) is based on all information of which preparer has any knowledge.

▶ Signature of general partner or limited liability company member manager ▶ Date

May the IRS discuss this return with the preparer shown below (see instructions)? ☐ Yes ☐ No

Paid Preparer Use Only	Print/Type preparer's name	Preparer's signature	Date	Check ☐ if self-employed	PTIN
	Firm's name ▶			Firm's EIN ▶	
	Firm's address ▶			Phone no.	

For Paperwork Reduction Act Notice, see separate instructions. Cat. No. 11390Z Form **1065** (2016)

Form K-1
Partner's Share of Current Year Income, Deductions, Credits and Other Items
Page 1 Only
For Form 1065 Partnership Return

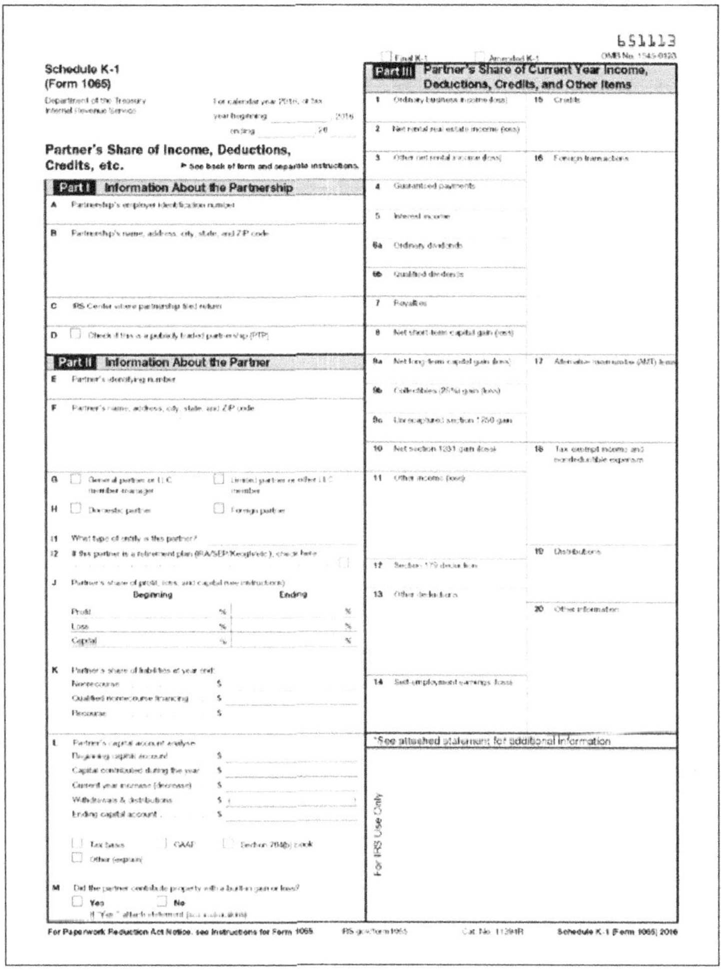

651113

☐ Final K-1 ☐ Amended K-1 OMB No. 1545-0123

Schedule K-1 (Form 1065)

Department of the Treasury
Internal Revenue Service

For calendar year 2016, or tax year beginning ______, 2016 ending ______, 20__

Partner's Share of Income, Deductions, Credits, etc. ► See back of form and separate instructions.

Part I Information About the Partnership

A Partnership's employer identification number

B Partnership's name, address, city, state, and ZIP code

C IRS Center where partnership filed return

D ☐ Check if this is a publicly traded partnership (PTP)

Part II Information About the Partner

E Partner's identifying number

F Partner's name, address, city, state, and ZIP code

G ☐ General partner or LLC member-manager ☐ Limited partner or other LLC member

H ☐ Domestic partner ☐ Foreign partner

I1 What type of entity is this partner?

I2 If this partner is a retirement plan (IRA/SEP/Keogh/etc.), check here ☐

J Partner's share of profit, loss, and capital (see instructions):

	Beginning	Ending
Profit	%	%
Loss	%	%
Capital	%	%

K Partner's share of liabilities at year end:

Nonrecourse $

Qualified nonrecourse financing $

Recourse $

L Partner's capital account analysis:

Beginning capital account $

Capital contributed during the year $

Current year increase (decrease) $

Withdrawals & distributions $ ( )

Ending capital account $

☐ Tax basis ☐ GAAP ☐ Section 704(b) book

☐ Other (explain)

M Did the partner contribute property with a built-in gain or loss?

☐ Yes ☐ No

If "Yes," attach statement (see instructions)

Part III Partner's Share of Current Year Income, Deductions, Credits, and Other Items

1 Ordinary business income (loss)

2 Net rental real estate income (loss)

3 Other net rental income (loss)

4 Guaranteed payments

5 Interest income

6a Ordinary dividends

6b Qualified dividends

7 Royalties

8 Net short-term capital gain (loss)

9a Net long-term capital gain (loss)

9b Collectibles (28%) gain (loss)

9c Unrecaptured section 1250 gain

10 Net section 1231 gain (loss)

11 Other income (loss)

12 Section 179 deduction

13 Other deductions

14 Self-employment earnings (loss)

15 Credits

16 Foreign transactions

17 Alternative minimum tax (AMT) items

18 Tax-exempt income and nondeductible expenses

19 Distributions

20 Other information

*See attached statement for additional information.

For IRS Use Only

For Paperwork Reduction Act Notice, see Instructions for Form 1065. IRS.gov/form1065 Cat. No. 11394R Schedule K-1 (Form 1065) 2016

Form 1120-C
Corporation Return
Page 1 Only

Form **1120** Department of the Treasury Internal Revenue Service

U.S. Corporation Income Tax Return

For calendar year 2016 or tax year beginning , 2016, ending , 20

▶ Information about Form 1120 and its separate instructions is at *www.irs.gov/form1120.*

OMB No. 1545-0123

A Check if:
1a Consolidated return (attach Form 851) ☐
b Life/nonlife consolidated return ☐
2 Personal holding co. (attach Sch. PH) ☐
3 Personal service corp. (see instructions) ☐
4 Schedule M-3 attached ☐

TYPE OR PRINT
Name
Number, street, and room or suite no. If a P.O. box, see instructions.
City or town, state, or province, country, and ZIP or foreign postal code

B Employer identification number
C Date incorporated
D Total assets (see instructions) $

E Check if: (1) ☐ Initial return (2) ☐ Final return (3) ☐ Name change (4) ☐ Address change

Income	1a	Gross receipts or sales	1a	
	b	Returns and allowances	1b	
	c	Balance. Subtract line 1b from line 1a		1c
	2	Cost of goods sold (attach Form 1125-A)		2
	3	Gross profit. Subtract line 2 from line 1c		3
	4	Dividends (Schedule C, line 19)		4
	5	Interest		5
	6	Gross rents		6
	7	Gross royalties		7
	8	Capital gain net income (attach Schedule D (Form 1120))		8
	9	Net gain or (loss) from Form 4797, Part II, line 17 (attach Form 4797)		9
	10	Other income (see instructions—attach statement)		10
	11	**Total income.** Add lines 3 through 10 ▶		11
Deductions (See instructions for limitations on deductions.)	12	Compensation of officers (see instructions—attach Form 1125-E) ▶		12
	13	Salaries and wages (less employment credits)		13
	14	Repairs and maintenance		14
	15	Bad debts		15
	16	Rents		16
	17	Taxes and licenses		17
	18	Interest		18
	19	Charitable contributions		19
	20	Depreciation from Form 4562 not claimed on Form 1125-A or elsewhere on return (attach Form 4562)		20
	21	Depletion		21
	22	Advertising		22
	23	Pension, profit-sharing, etc., plans		23
	24	Employee benefit programs		24
	25	Domestic production activities deduction (attach Form 8903)		25
	26	Other deductions (attach statement)		26
	27	**Total deductions.** Add lines 12 through 26 ▶		27
	28	Taxable income before net operating loss deduction and special deductions. Subtract line 27 from line 11		28
	29a	Net operating loss deduction (see instructions)	29a	
	b	Special deductions (Schedule C, line 20)	29b	
	c	Add lines 29a and 29b		29c
Tax, Refundable Credits, and Payments	30	**Taxable income.** Subtract line 29c from line 28. See instructions		30
	31	Total tax (Schedule J, Part I, line 11)		31
	32	Total payments and refundable credits (Schedule J, Part II, line 21)		32
	33	Estimated tax penalty. See instructions. Check if Form 2220 is attached ▶ ☐		33
	34	**Amount owed.** If line 32 is smaller than the total of lines 31 and 33, enter amount owed		34
	35	**Overpayment.** If line 32 is larger than the total of lines 31 and 33, enter amount overpaid		35
	36	Enter amount from line 35 you want: **Credited to 2017 estimated tax ▶** **Refunded ▶**		36

Sign Here Under penalties of perjury, I declare that I have examined this return, including accompanying schedules and statements, and to the best of my knowledge and belief, it is true, correct, and complete. Declaration of preparer (other than taxpayer) is based on all information of which preparer has any knowledge.

▶ Signature of officer Date ▶ Title

May the IRS discuss this return with the preparer shown below? See instructions. ☐ **Yes** ☐ **No**

Paid Preparer Use Only
Print/Type preparer's name | Preparer's signature | Date | Check ☐ if self-employed | PTIN
Firm's name ▶ | Firm's EIN ▶
Firm's address ▶ | Phone no.

For Paperwork Reduction Act Notice, see separate instructions. Cat. No. 11450Q Form **1120** (2016)

Form 1120S
S Corporation Return
Page 1 Only

Form **1120S**

Department of the Treasury
Internal Revenue Service

U.S. Income Tax Return for an S Corporation

▶ Do not file this form unless the corporation has filed or is attaching Form 2553 to elect to be an S corporation.

▶ Information about Form 1120S and its separate instructions is at *www.irs.gov/form1120s*.

OMB No. 1545-0123

For calendar year 2016 or tax year beginning , 2016, ending , 20

A S election effective date

B Business activity code number (see instructions)

C Check if Sch. M-3 attached

TYPE OR PRINT — Name; Number, street, and room or suite no. If a P.O. box, see instructions.; City or town, state or province, country, and ZIP or foreign postal code

D Employer identification number

E Date incorporated

F Total assets (see instructions) $

G Is the corporation electing to be an S corporation beginning with this tax year? ☐ Yes ☐ No If "Yes," attach Form 2553 if not already filed

H Check if: (1) ☐ Final return (2) ☐ Name change (3) ☐ Address change (4) ☐ Amended return (5) ☐ S election termination or revocation

I Enter the number of shareholders who were shareholders during any part of the tax year ▶

Caution: Include **only** trade or business income and expenses on lines 1a through 21. See the instructions for more information.

Income	1a	Gross receipts or sales	1a
	b	Returns and allowances	1b
	c	Balance. Subtract line 1b from line 1a	1c
	2	Cost of goods sold (attach Form 1125-A)	2
	3	Gross profit. Subtract line 2 from line 1c	3
	4	Net gain (loss) from Form 4797, line 17 (attach Form 4797)	4
	5	Other income (loss) (see instructions—attach statement)	5
	6	**Total income (loss).** Add lines 3 through 5 ▶	6
Deductions (see instructions for limitations)	7	Compensation of officers (see instructions—attach Form 1125-E)	7
	8	Salaries and wages (less employment credits)	8
	9	Repairs and maintenance	9
	10	Bad debts	10
	11	Rents	11
	12	Taxes and licenses	12
	13	Interest	13
	14	Depreciation not claimed on Form 1125-A or elsewhere on return (attach Form 4562)	14
	15	Depletion **(Do not deduct oil and gas depletion.)**	15
	16	Advertising	16
	17	Pension, profit-sharing, etc., plans	17
	18	Employee benefit programs	18
	19	Other deductions (attach statement)	19
	20	**Total deductions.** Add lines 7 through 19 ▶	20
	21	**Ordinary business income (loss).** Subtract line 20 from line 6	21
Tax and Payments	22a	Excess net passive income or LIFO recapture tax (see instructions)	22a
	b	Tax from Schedule D (Form 1120S)	22b
	c	Add lines 22a and 22b (see instructions for additional taxes)	22c
	23a	2016 estimated tax payments and 2015 overpayment credited to 2016	23a
	b	Tax deposited with Form 7004	23b
	c	Credit for federal tax paid on fuels (attach Form 4136)	23c
	d	Add lines 23a through 23c	23d
	24	Estimated tax penalty (see instructions). Check if Form 2220 is attached ▶ ☐	24
	25	**Amount owed.** If line 23d is smaller than the total of lines 22c and 24, enter amount owed	25
	26	**Overpayment.** If line 23d is larger than the total of lines 22c and 24, enter amount overpaid	26
	27	Enter amount from line 26 **Credited to 2017 estimated tax** ▶ **Refunded** ▶	27

Sign Here — Under penalties of perjury, I declare that I have examined this return, including accompanying schedules and statements, and to the best of my knowledge and belief, it is true, correct, and complete. Declaration of preparer (other than taxpayer) is based on all information of which preparer has any knowledge.

▶ Signature of officer — Date — ▶ Title

May the IRS discuss this return with the preparer shown below (see instructions)? ☐ Yes ☐ No

Paid Preparer Use Only — Print/Type preparer's name — Preparer's signature — Date — Check ☐ if self-employed — PTIN

Firm's name ▶ — Firm's EIN ▶

Firm's address ▶ — Phone no.

For Paperwork Reduction Act Notice, see separate instructions. Cat. No. 11510H Form **1120S** (2016)

Form K-1
Shareholder's Share of Current Year Income, Deductions, Credits and Other Items
Page 1 Only
For Form 1120S S Corporation Return

671113

☐ Final K-1 ☐ Amended K-1 OMB No. 1545-0123

Schedule K-1 (Form 1120S) 2016
Department of the Treasury
Internal Revenue Service

For calendar year 2016, or tax year beginning ________, 2016 ending ________, 20____

Shareholder's Share of Income, Deductions, Credits, etc. ► See back of form and separate instructions.

Part I Information About the Corporation

A Corporation's employer identification number

B Corporation's name, address, city, state, and ZIP code

C IRS Center where corporation filed return

Part II Information About the Shareholder

D Shareholder's identifying number

E Shareholder's name, address, city, state, and ZIP code

F Shareholder's percentage of stock ownership for tax year ________ %

For IRS Use Only

Part III Shareholder's Share of Current Year Income, Deductions, Credits, and Other Items

1	Ordinary business income (loss)	13	Credits
2	Net rental real estate income (loss)		
3	Other net rental income (loss)		
4	Interest income		
5a	Ordinary dividends		
5b	Qualified dividends	14	Foreign transactions
6	Royalties		
7	Net short-term capital gain (loss)		
8a	Net long-term capital gain (loss)		
8b	Collectibles (28%) gain (loss)		
8c	Unrecaptured section 1250 gain		
9	Net section 1231 gain (loss)		
10	Other income (loss)	15	Alternative minimum tax (AMT) items
11	Section 179 deduction	16	Items affecting shareholder basis
12	Other deductions		
		17	Other information

* See attached statement for additional information.

For Paperwork Reduction Act Notice, see Instructions for Form 1120S. IRS.gov/form1120s Cat. No. 11520D **Schedule K-1 (Form 1120S) 2016**

About the Author

Tax Larry M. Weinstein is a CPA (Texas) and Certified Tax Reduction Strategist® from Houston, Texas.

He is the Managing Director of CertifiedTaxReductionStrategist.com.

Larry graduated from the University of Houston with a BBA in Accounting and began his career in the Houston office of Arthur Young, now known as Ernst & Young.

In private practice since 1988, Larry concentrates in the area of Strategic Tax Planning, mostly for closely held businesses.

Larry has worked with hundreds of individuals and business owners through the years, helping them to legally lower their taxes and stay compliant with the IRS rules and regulations.

Larry is the developer of the Strategic Tax Reduction Process™.

Larry lives in Houston with his wife and two daughters. When he is not spending time with his family or watching his daughter compete in college gymnastics (go Texas State Bobcats!!), he enjoys riding his recumbent tricycle and bicycle, and photography.

Made in United States
North Haven, CT
04 November 2026

21763953R00055